your Dream Handbook

your Dream Handbook

UNLOCK THE MEANING OF YOUR DREAMS TO CHANGE YOUR LIFE

marc j. gian

CICO BOOKS

LONDON NEW YORK

This book is dedicated to my niece, Abigail, and nephew, Kevin, as I hope that they will be able to find inspiration from it in years to come. Their questions about night dreams at such young ages encourages me that this book is needed.

This edition published in 2024 by CICO Books
An imprint of Ryland Peters & Small Ltd
20–21 Jockey's Fields   341 E 116th St
London WC1R 4BW   New York, NY 10029

www.rylandpeters.com

10 9 8 7 6 5 4 3 2 1

First published in 2019 as *The Inner World of Night Dreams*

A CIP catalog record for this book is available from the Library of Congress and the British Library.

ISBN: 978-1-80065-339-9

Printed in China

Editor: Clare Churly
Illustrator: Sarah Perkins

Commissioning editor: Kristine Pidkameny
Art director: Sally Powell
Production controller: David Hearn
Publishing manager: Penny Craig
Publisher: Cindy Richards

contents

introduction

For as long as I can remember, I have always aimed to live in truth and freedom while staying connected to the invisible reality. Although the truth was painful at times, it was meaningful for growth, and it propelled me to study the healing arts, starting at the age of eighteen. After spending over twenty years working in the field of health and assisting others in wellbeing, I have found that dreamwork is the most potent tool for self-discovery. It is essential for those who want to foster a deeper and more honest connection with themselves, and create lasting changes both in themselves and in their relationships.

In 2004, I met Dr. Peter Reznik, who became my mentor in mind-body integration and bestowed, taught, and shared the wisdom of Mind-Body Integrative Therapy, as taught to him by the Jewish sage Colette Aboulker-Muscat. From that time onward the principles of Mind-Body Integrative Therapy have been at the forefront of my personal spiritual practice and have provided a guiding light for my work with clients.

This book is about using your dreams to achieve self-mastery and walk the path of truth. It outlines the integrated mental tools and specific mind-body principles that are needed to immerse yourself in the pictorial language of dreams. Countless books, articles, and research papers about dreams have been published, but this book is so much more than just another publication on the subject. Here you will learn the specific principles of mind-body integration that can be implemented every day for healing, with or without dreamwork. You will come to understand that your dreams are calling upon you—and, sometimes, even begging or nagging you—to work with them. You will discover that your dreams are a reflection of you, and that they are asking you, sometimes kindly and sometimes boldly, to interact with them upon awakening.

Dreams are our best and most powerful teachers, always one step ahead of the conscious mind. They have the power to give us clarity and freedom, but only if we listen. There are various types of dream, including meeting dreams, precognitive dreams, prophetic dreams, intuitive dreams, historical dreams, and lucid dreams (see page 128 for more information about types of dream). In this book, my focus is on wisdom dreams: the dreams that embody our past, our present, and possibilities for our future. They are a powerful tool for self-discovery and personal transcendence, allowing us to connect to the part of ourselves that has access to the whole of ourselves.

Dreamwork, or working with night dreams, can act as a catalyst for expanding awareness of the self and its surroundings, which is key to opening the doors of truth. We are all born with full potential, yet sometimes, as life unfolds, we realize that we have not fulfilled (or are not fulfilling) that potential. Some reasons for this failure to fulfill our potential may include false beliefs and holding on to negative experiences or emotional factors. Working with wisdom dreams and mental imagery will allow you to begin to access your daily potential, and to achieve personal goals as you move through obstacles.

This book contains a seed of potential and possibility, and it is up to you to water it and allow it to grow into a path of healing and decision-making. It is my hope that the words and exercises in the pages ahead will infuse you with the inspiration, insight, and confidence necessary to move forward in life, break away and/or integrate aspects from your past, reach your brightest potential, fulfill your divine destiny, and unlock your dormant gifts. In other words, develop the ability to be present to who you really are.

chapter 1

foundations for working with night dreams

Dreamwork is one modality under the umbrella of Mind-Body Integrative Therapy. In this chapter, we are going to build the foundations for dreamwork. You will discover the principles and methods of mind-body integration and learn about the images and who is who in your dreams. As with anything new, allow yourself to be open to fresh ideas. The healing keystones outlined in this chapter are not only suitable for dreamwork but also foundational principles for living a full and integrated life; they will expand the way you view and experience your personal life and your relationships. Let the journey begin...

mind–body integration

Mind–Body Integrative Therapy is a millennia-old tradition that originated in the Mediterranean. Rooted in ancient healing principles, it recognizes the interplay between mind, body, and soul and our ability to use free will to align with the best of ourselves. It is an approach to healing that acknowledges that the invisible (function) creates the visible (form). This means that our belief precedes our experience, and our experience is simply an outward manifestation of our beliefs or issues in life that need to be addressed.

All aspects of our physical body have meaning. Therefore, in order to fully treat an ailment, we must look at the meaning of the disease and the part of the body that is being affected. Mind–Body Integrative Therapy is grounded in the belief that our mind is an integral element in our journey to healing, and that through intention and will we can make any necessary corrections.

We all have aspects of ourselves that we would like to complete or make whole. Mind–body integration can assist us in fulfilling that unused potential. Whether the issue is physical, mental, or emotional, the practice of mind–body integration will allow us to examine the situation as a whole and use our beliefs and desires to resolve the problem.

the five principles of mind–body integration

I have organized some of the basic principles of mind–body integration below. Once you understand them you can begin to use them in your daily life—there is no need to wait for your dreams. By implementing these principles in your everyday life, you can begin to live with more freedom and self-authority.

"That which is Below corresponds to that which is Above, and that which is Above corresponds to that which is Below..."

THE EMERALD TABLET

1 AS ABOVE, SO BELOW:
the mind and body influence each other

Above us there is truth, and below (in the physical world) we get to experience that truth in our daily lives. In other words, our lives "below" animate the possibilities that come from "above" (the cosmic consciousness).

Disease, health, and possible attitudes all come from "above" (the mind, which is more than just the brain and encompasses the spirit), and are experienced "below" (in the physical body). If this seems contrary to what you believe, let's take a deeper look. The terms "above" and "below" signify that life has a vertical axis. What is to be experienced in this world comes from "above." We can think of this as a guiding light from the "above." In addition, we are all made in the image of the Creator; therefore, we must all be creators in many aspects of our lives. Finally, it's important to understand that the microcosm and the macrocosm are reflections of each other. Therefore, as the microcosm reflects the macrocosm, and as we are created in the image of the Creator, our minds ("above") have the ability to create, affecting our bodies ("below") and our experiences.

What happens in the physical realm is an effect, or mirror, of the influence from above. We can think of this as the mind affecting the body and our emotions. A simple exercise of memory recall can prove how the mind and body influence each other. Take a moment to imagine a negative experience from your past. How does it feel in your body? Does your mood change? Now imagine a positive event from your past. Does it feel different?

Just as the "above" affects the "below," so the "below," too, can affect the "above." This is one of the purposes of prayer. Whatever exists in the spiritual realm is also in the physical realm. When we make corrections in our personal life ("below"), blessings come from "above." Similarly, setting your intentions in the physical world will change your mental and emotional state, thereby changing the blueprint for the days ahead.

The axiom "as above, so below" indicates that the spiritual realm is the vertical axis and we are here to animate it on the horizontal axis (the physical realm). Our physical form indicates a vertical axis: we stand upright on two feet with the help of our spine to ascend. Healing is also on a vertical axis. If disease, health, and experience come from "above," what is the best way to heal or transform? You guessed it: from "below to above" or "above to below."

Rabbi Nachman of Breslov taught that imagination is highest in the physical realm and lowest in the spiritual realm. Imagination is in the mind, which is "above," and after an imagery exercise or dreamwork, we bring it back down into our emotional physical being. When we go deep within our being, we bring our imagination back up or down to the physical. We experience intuition, spirituality, emotions, feelings, energy fields, and vibrational healing all on the vertical axis. Ideas come from "above," and we can choose to bring them down and implant them in the horizontal physical world. In the coming chapters, you will learn the tools to do this through your night dreams.

2 FUNCTION COMES BEFORE FORM:
the invisible creates the visible

In order for something to come into form, two key things need to happen: there needs to be an idea from "above" (cosmic consciousness and the mind) to fulfill a function for our physical world, and there needs to be an action from "below" (in the physical world) to put it into form. There are examples all around us. Take the chair you are sitting on, for instance. What is its function? Its function is to make you more comfortable when sitting. A clock's function is to tell time. A refrigerator's function is to keep food fresh. Even something as simple as the handle on a coffee mug serves a purpose. The same applies to the physical body. Each part of the body has a function before the form. For example, the heart, for many, reflects love and compassion; the liver and gallbladder reflect anger and direction; the legs reflect the direction we are going to go; the eyes mirror sight; and the ears are made to hear the sounds of the world.

The idea that function precedes form also relates to our relationships. Take a few moments now to notice what you are receiving from and giving to your relationships. Ask yourself which relationships are serving your deepest purpose and which are not. Each relationship can function as a learning tool for your own self-discovery.

Perhaps, on a deeper level, this book on dreams serves a function because there is a need for people to align themselves with their truest purpose. Everything and every relationship has a function for you.

3 BELIEF CREATES OUR EXPERIENCE:
we are all in the process of becoming

For many, this principle can be challenging at first, yet quite rewarding over time. Why? If you change a belief, you can alter the course of your life and your destiny. When we are born, we inherit energies from ancestral experiences, beliefs, and even certain "soul corrections" (the opportunity to overcome our physical nature and our negative inclinations during this life's trials and tribulations). Usually, we are given the opportunity to make three to five major soul corrections here on Earth. If the "above" is not part of your belief system, no problem; the "below" may be better suited for you.

Most of our beliefs exist in our subconscious, which acts as a storage point for everyday information and memories. Many of us are not in touch with what we believe because we are unsure of who we are, or because we do not take the time to sit with ourselves. On the other hand, some of us attain a deeper understanding of self but choose to keep that knowledge hidden. It is as if our unconscious thoughts are planting seeds in our subconscious mind, resulting in an experience. Take a moment to reflect on current or past situations in your life and ask yourself what belief about yourself or the world you needed (or need) to have for each experience.

If belief creates experience, our interactions with other people are meetings of consciousness. Has anyone ever stolen from you? Did you feel like a victim afterward? Now, what if you looked at this incident from the perspective that belief creates experience? This implies that there is something within you that allowed the stealing to happen. Of course, this does not make the thief's action just, but if you can see that your mind/belief played a core part in the experience then you can change the belief.

Any experience is a meeting of minds, allowing for awareness. All experiences are purposeful because they reflect back on who we are. By mindfully making corrections to your beliefs, you are allowing yourself to become the hero, the king, or the queen of your life. Wisdom and growth can be attained from any situation. To live as if belief creates our experience is what the psychiatrist Gerald Epstein calls "the first big step in personal salvation."

4. THE LAW OF RECIPROCITY
change the inner to change the outer/change the outer to change the inner

There is an old adage, "G-d helps those who help themselves." When an individual puts in the effort to make a shift, the formless world sends help. Many of us may not realize that we depend upon the world above to achieve in this world. Ask yourself what you have been sending out energetically with your emotions and thoughts. What stories do you have in your mind that are being reflected in your experience? Do you, like many people, have "negative self-talk?" If so, is it serving you? If not, keep reading because you will find tools and techniques for "positive self-talk" and learn how to emody a new and positive way of being (see Mental Imagery, page 19).

Each thought you have carries an image, and each image contains energy. The combination of thought, image, belief, and emotions is a formula for creation. You will soon discover that the images you are holding are at least partly responsible for your experience in this world.

5. IMAGES ARE BOTH QUALITIES AND EMBODIMENTS OF THE INNER SELF

Imagery is the true universal language and with dreamwork you are in direct contact with it. It is imperative to understand that the images we encounter in our dreams are manifestations of our selves—likenesses of the self and/or stories of past experiences. Why stories of past experiences? Well, that's because when we have a particularly positive or negative experience, we usually continue to think about it—creating a narrative. The emotions we experience become a part of us, and they are reflected in areas of our life, whether or not we are aware of it. Such emotions may become a part of us, but that doesn't mean we are our emotions. Images can also reflect our beliefs, our attitudes, and the state and quality of our physical and emotional health.

Images come from the invisible and limitless imaginal realm "above." The imaginal realm is the nonmaterial realm of existence that includes thoughts, desires, and all else that is creative before it comes into physical existence. The imaginal realm is closer to the source of creation than our physical world is. Yet when we access the

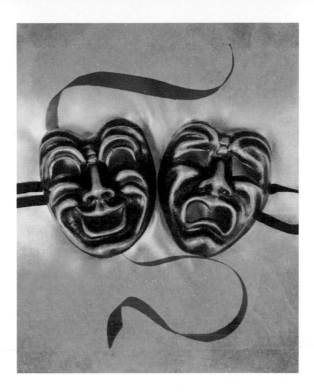

imaginal realm through imagery, we can still see, taste, feel, and hear. The number of available images from the imaginal realm is limitless—they are being created at every moment.

Images contain a more complete story than our verbal language has the ability to define. In the coming chapters you will experience the value of exploring images with both mental imagery and dreamwork. This process will depict where you are presently (mentally and emotionally), and you will learn how to make changes in your daily life by modifying those images to your liking.

You will soon discover that the images you are holding are at least partly responsible for your experience in this world.

methods of mind–body integration

The main modalities of mind–body integration are morphology (face reading), mental imagery, and dreamwork.

facial morphology

Facial morphology, or face reading, is the study of the human face and how it depicts personality and emotional and mental tendencies. The prefix "morph" means "form," and the suffix "ology" means "to study."

Our facial features disclose and represent our innate constitution and temperament. In other words, our inner world is reflected on our face. Most of our personal tendencies, including temperament, constitution, emotions, and even the inherent beliefs and issues we need to work through in life, are shown in the bone structure of our profile. However, our profile does not account for all our tendencies. The front view of our face is connected to our persona or what we show to the world or, in other words, how we appear to others.

By understanding the four different facial structures that are seen in our profile (sanguine, nervous, lymphatic, and bilious), along with twelve face shapes, we can discern the best diet for an individual, the best type and amount of physical exercise, the ideal partner, and more. Since our faces reveal so much, perhaps we are not as clothed as we think we are while in public.

While we don't need to learn face reading to advance in dreamwork, it is important to acknowledge that our face is a reflection of our inner world and how we relate to ourselves and the environment. This is also a great example of how function precedes form: as our face shows our tendencies in the waking world, so it shares our tendencies in the mirror/reflection of the dream world. Therefore, if you learn facial morphology you will have a better understanding of the information in your dreams. Also, if you understand that we are all born with a specific temperament and constitution, you can begin to live with less judgment and more freedom, as you know what you are working with in this life.

mental imagery

Imagery is the primary language of humans. Before babies can understand verbal language, they perceive, interact with, and accumulate images. Even when we grow up and use linear verbal language, we still use imagery.

Verbal language comes via the intellect. It is beneficial for communicating facts and instructions, such as how to bake a cake or to give directions to someone. However, when we engage in imagery and dreamwork, we use a pictorial (or imaginal) language. This language of images is the true universal language, and some people believe that it is more powerful than verbal language.

Consider, for example, a word in a dictionary. When you look at the word you will see the individual letters that make up the spelling of that word; yet, in your inner mind you will also see an image. For example, when I think of the word "dog," I immediately picture my dog, Tia. Perhaps the word "rainbow" will make you think of a time where you experienced a magnificent rainbow, or the word "house" will transport you to a specific house. Think about your favorite song. Do you see the written lyrics in your mind or an array of images, emotions, and sounds that come from your memory of that tune?

The images you experience are unique to you. They do not come from your outside world but from your inner one. They are formed by your beliefs, your experiences, and your genetic makeup. Why is this important? Because when we use the tool of mental imagery, we are going inward to find truth and meaning.

Mental imagery is a special healing tool that enables exploration and discovery of truth. It can be used to heal and redesign emotional, mental, and physical states. During mental imagery, an imaginer may use all their senses (seeing, feeling, tasting, smelling, hearing, and intuition), and use their intention to shift inward and see and experience the issues within the body. For example, if one of my clients feels that an issue is emotional, I will ask them where they feel it in their body, then direct them to set the intention to bring consciousness to the area and have them share what it is they see. Then we will try to discover the underlying cause and, if desired, transform the image.

It must be noted that there is a difference between mental imagery and just using your imagination. With mental imagery there is a clear intention, direction, and focus on what to change or what to see. Imagination is more like daydreaming; it does not have intentionality, direction, or focus.

The use of proper mental imagery is integral for people who are seeking success in particular areas of life, such as their career or relationships. It can help them work with beliefs that may be shaping their life experience. Mental imagery can also be used when going to a stressful event, such as a speaking engagement, a meeting, seeing family or in-laws over the holidays, or starting a new career.

One area where the tool of mental imagery is particularly effective is when dealing with seemingly negative emotional or physical experiences that have not been integrated. It is not necessary to give examples here; all we need to do is take a glimpse into our memories and we soon become aware of those that bring up emotions such as fear, anxiety, and anger. When doing mental imagery, we can move toward the remembered scene and transform it to our liking, which can lead to a positive difference in our mental, emotional, and physical being. Using this tool does not change the past event, but it can transform the feeling you have from it, allowing you to live life with more freedom.

Like an artist, you can use your own pictorial language
to create art, and the beauty of this approach is
that you can erase your own art too.

When using mental imagery, I tend to ask my clients to explain the situation to me as if I were a young child, which makes them more likely to use images, or I will simply ask them to describe the situation with an image. Below are some examples:

- I feel like a small ant when I am at work.
- I feel I am living under a rock, with no social life.
- I feel like I am in jail.
- I am always in the corner.
- I am boxed in.
- My head is spinning.
- There is a knife in my heart.
- I am weighed down.
- I am so much lighter; the weight has been lifted.
- My heart is wide open.
- I am grounded.

WHAT IS AN IMAGE?

In *Waking Dream Therapy: Dream Process as Imagination,* Gerald Epstein states that "images are the concretizations of emotions" and that the "exploration of the imaginal realm is, in effect, the immersion of oneself in emotion." Images are the embodiments of qualities within ourselves. This book will focus on how night dreams and images work in the same way.

Most of us do not realize that when we are thinking it is with images. Put down this book for about a minute and just begin to "think." Can you describe what you were thinking? Were you thinking in words or was it mostly in images and moving scenes? A single image can communicate a whole story. Like an artist, you can use your own pictorial language to create art, and the beauty of this approach is that you can erase your own art too.

Pictorial language conveys emotions, actions, and meaning, and creates instantaneous recognition. A good example of a universal image is the envelope symbol that signifies email. If you show an image of an envelope to someone who does not speak the same verbal language, it is likely they will have an idea of what it is. But if you show them the letters "E M A I L" they may not understand. A traffic light is another example of a universal image that conveys appropriate action. Pictorial language does not need words to convey its meaning, although during imagery and dreams we often do use verbal language.

WHAT IS THE VALUE OF CHANGING AN IMAGE?

One of the benefits of working with images is that it allows the practitioner to move through an imaginary process that is real. During an imagery exercise the imaginer can feel, see, hear, and acknowledge that the image or scene is an embodiment within them, and take responsibility for their part (own it). Then, when transforming the image to one of their liking, which again can include feeling, seeing, and hearing, they change the embodiment within them and begin to change the path of experience for the days ahead.

When we transform images or scenes in a dream, we are correcting qualities, emotions, behaviors, and even physical illnesses. Experiencing the image or scene of images is imperative, as we need to take responsibility for an experience in order to disown it. When we move through this process, we are allowing our being to spontaneously connect to our "higher self." Imaginal work allows a person to see the totality of a situation. It is a gift that continues to unwrap over time.

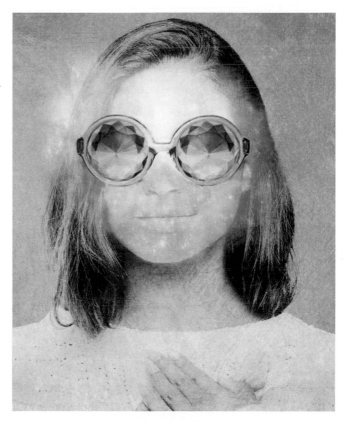

It is important to note that in your imagination anything is possible. You can become your own superhero, your own liberator, your

own healer. Mental imagery grants the imaginer the opportunity to go inside a conflict and use imagery to transform conflict into peace. This process happens because the imaginer is using their own consciousness to change an experience. The key is to go into the conflict. If you try to sidestep the inner conflict, it may just keep on growing—the only way out is through.

Since we are working with the idea that belief creates experience, changing images in dreams and during mental imagery exercises may be the key to unlocking the door to a better reality. However, first you need to own the qualities you want to change:

• If you see yourself as a coward, you can move toward courage.

• If you are angry, you can move toward love and acceptance.

• If you see yourself in a maze (lacking direction), you can find your direction and get out.

• If you see yourself in jail (perhaps you feel guilty about something), you can break free and choose to live in freedom. (If you feel a true guilt, commit to not doing that action again.)

• If you see yourself as a fearful child, you can speak to the child and offer encouragement.

- If you see a knife in your back or abdomen (perhaps you have been deceived recently), you can work to transform this image.

- If you have a job interview or a meeting soon, see how you feel it is going to go and transform the experience to one of confidence, strength, and fun.

- If you are still holding on to a past relationship, ask yourself whether you are ready to let go and move on. Say goodbye.

- If you are in physical pain, move your mind inward and see how the image corresponds to your emotions, beliefs, or experiences. What is the texture? What is the color? Is it dry or wet?

Whatever the image you see, own it and then disown it by creating a new image!

Remember the definition of images: they are the embodiment of emotions, experiences, and beliefs. Changing images grants us the opportunity to transform inner conflicts into new experiences. By changing images, we are activating our intention and using our will to live in greater congruence with the world around us.

WILL I BENEFIT FROM WORKING WITH MENTAL IMAGES?

Ask yourself:

- Are there any areas of your life that you want to shift?

- Do you have a potentially stressful event coming up?

- Have you ever wondered what it would be like to live life with full confidence?

- Are you lacking will and perseverance?

- Have you ever woken from a dream and said to yourself, "Thank G-d, it was just a dream!"?

If you answered yes to any of these questions, mental imagery and dreamwork may be the key to living in a new reality of your own making. Keep reading!

dreamwork

Dreamwork is a modality that uses mental imagery upon awakening to change the dream and enhance and change the direction of one's life. It uses pictorial (or imaginal) language (see page 19, Mental Imagery) to discover truths in all aspects of one's life.

Dreams depict our personal, cultural, and religious beliefs; our emotional and physical challenges; and our relationships with ourselves, others, and the environment. Dreams provide answers to present situations in our waking life (although it is up to us to follow through on that advice). It is easier to make a decision following a dream because we have touched the non-linear, non-judgmental aspect of ourselves. In this way, night dreams act as a catalyst for changing our waking life.

KEY CONCEPTS OF DREAMWORK

Dreamwork explores the meaning of dreams on the basis that each person's dreams are unique, and therefore the individual meanings are unique. The term "dreamwork" implies two processes that come together. Simply speaking, we experience one or many dreams every night, and in the morning we uncover the meaning and consider how it reflects and parallels our waking life. Webster's Dictionary defines work as an "activity involving mental or physical effort done in order to achieve a purpose or result." Working with dreams will take effort—a concerted effort between you and your soul. This work will prepare for an expansion of your awareness and the ability to live a grounded and spiritual life.

night dreams are a mirror of waking life

When we work with our night dreams, we are looking into our reflection, for night dreams are a mirror of our waking world. Journeying into dreams allows the dreamer to witness and learn more about not only their immediate self but also what is happening around them. This is possible because the "ego" is not present, our defenses are not present, and we are in a boundless reality. Unlike the waking world, our dreams are limitless in their possibilities.

Dreams come to us as a reflection aligning the dreamer to the current situations they experience in daily life. Once we begin to work with night dreams, we start to

Dreams come to us as a reflection aligning the dreamer
to the current situations they experience in daily life.

experience this alignment and even begin to see correspondences in our waking life. For example, I worked with a client who had a dream in which a racehorse wearing a saddlecloth with the number four won a race; and the next day he drove through a toll booth with the number four. The starting gate for the race in the dream looked similar to a toll booth. This may sound silly, but this is the type of synchronicity (coincidental occurrence) that begins to occur when you work with your dreams. At the time he had this dream about the racehorse, he was also heading into a new romantic relationship. What does a relationship have to do with this dream? Well, the number four is the number connected to home and marriage. Ultimately this relationship did not lead to marriage, but it was significant in his life. Perhaps the dream was showing him that he was rushing into something. Why? It was a race. You can learn more about seeing synchronicities in your waking life based on the numbers and colors that appear in your dreams on pages 41 and 43.

Every dream is unique to its dreamer—belief, experience, culture, and cultural history all play a role in the dream experience. This book will explore how the images and experiences within night dreams are personal to you, yet share universal concepts with those of other dreamers. After all, we are all human, we all move through similar circumstances in life, and we all have aspects of our life that we are trying to integrate, past experiences that need to be resolved, and future desires, dreams, and goals with the potential to become reality.

Through specific steps, we can mine the wisdom of our dreams. In order to do this, we need to activate our intention and willpower (invisible) and take action (visible).

Dreamwork acts as a vehicle that, if driven correctly, will transport the dreamer to freedom, new discoveries, and new perceptions.

your body reacts to dreams

At times your physical body will react to what is happening in a dream. For example, when you have a nightmare, you may wake up sweating, with palpitations and fear. During REM sleep (the sleep phase when we are having most of our dreams) it is now believed that the neurotransmitters gamma-aminobutyric acid (GABA) and glycine temporarily paralyze the skeletal muscles to prevent us from acting out what is happening in our dreams. However, you are always where your mind is. When you wake from a dream, ask yourself where you just were. Were you lying in bed or were you in the dream world?

everyone dreams

Many people claim that they do not dream or do not remember their dreams. Well, the truth is that we all dream. For those of us who do not remember our dreams, there are external and internal tools can be used to support the remembering of dreams. We will learn more about this on page 60.

KEY ATTITUDES OF DREAMWORK

A positive, open, and receptive mind will bring forth the benefits of working with night dreams. Below are some essential attitudes that are universal in their application, meaning you don't need to focus on all of them for one to be effective. If you're integrating these attitudes into other areas of your life, you will notice positive mental and emotional changes during your day.

honesty

We are all in the process of becoming. We all have similar lessons to learn in life. We all have our strengths and weaknesses. Simply put, we are all in this together.

When people start to do dreamwork with me, I ask them where in their lives they feel conflicted or troubled. They will usually say one or two things. Since two is the number of conflict, if they offer two answers, I ask them for a third. Often they say in a soft voice that they do not know. As they begin to look down, I know they have got something. And I proceed, saying, "If you have one more, you can choose to let me know so that we can go deeper and you can get even more out of the dream, or you can keep it to yourself." I've never had anyone keep it to themselves!

Shame and guilt are two emotions that discourage us from revealing honest thoughts, and most often they are not a true shame or a real guilt. We are all human and have all made mistakes. Remember, you are getting to know yourself and this process can lead to a greater love for yourself. It is also important to be honest about what you want in life.

openness

Be open to the process of becoming aware that there is much more to this life than the physical. As an idea, try out a few of the principles of mind-body integration every day for a few days, following the plan outlined below. Keep a written note of your experiences in a dream journal (see page 66).

• **Day 1 (belief creates our experience):** Ask yourself about a past experience. It could be, for example, not being able to pay bills; being able to live a financially successful life; difficulty finding a relationship; having a fulfilling relationship; not being able to share what is on your mind; being able share what's on your mind; staying in a job environment that is not healthy; or having a healthy working environment. What belief do you need in order to have such an experience? Additionally, ask yourself what experience you want and what belief you need to have to achieve it.

• **Day 2 (as above, so below):** Sit in a comfortable position. Take a few slow and relaxed breaths, always exhaling more than you inhale, then imagine a very positive experience in your life. It could be the time you met your partner, graduated from school, or saw your favorite band for the first time. Stay in this moment for 18 seconds. Notice how you feel. Where do you feel it? Can you see how your mind ("above") affects your body ("below")?

• **Day 3 (function comes before form):** Notice the world around you. What is the function of the form in your space?

• **Day 4 (the law of reciprocity):** Make an effort to change something about your life, and examine how you feel. Perhaps you need to exercise, eat healthily, do something creative, or simply pray or say a mantra, such as, "As I change my inner

Remember, you are getting to know yourself and this process can lead to a greater love for yourself.

thought, my outer world will change." Whenever you catch yourself saying something negative about yourself, say, "Whoops! There I go again!" and then tell yourself the exact opposite.

self-acceptance

We are all born with qualities that we appreciate in ourselves, but we also are born with traits that are not to our liking. In order to disown anything, we must first own it. If you believe in G-d or a Creator, this part becomes much easier, because the "above" created you with what you perceive as your weaknesses or challenges. Accept that life has given you what you need to complete your mission here while in a physical form.

compassion

Developing compassion allows us to see and experience the greater landscape of our life through a wider lens, freeing us of judgmental attitudes toward ourselves and others. To develop compassion, look inward and be loving of yourself and where you are in life. We all move through our fair share of trials and tribulations.

Compassion clears the way for love and action, which is an asset when we encounter people not to our liking in our dreams. In your waking life, too, the people you have an aversion to may be a reflection of personal qualities. I know there have been times in my life when I could not stand another person, but once I started to see similarities between the two of us, and accepted them, our relationship transformed.

courage

The process of healing takes courage. When doing this work, we are bound to come across things we fear, whether it's a quality of our self, an image, or a scene in the dream. Know that you have it within you to become the hero of any situation.

When you wake from an unsettling dream where you were chased by a bear, or encountered someone you fear, or were walking down a dark alley, feel the fear of the dream experience. Upon awakening, know that it is your turn to overcome fear and be the hero of your dream!

connection

When we have night dreams we are connecting to a greater and more aware part of ourselves. Upon awakening, we have a golden opportunity to link our dream to our waking life, forging a deeper connection to our whole self.

trust

Dreamwork is a tool for self-discovery, but we cannot discover or uncover everything in one night. Trust the process. Becoming a master of your dreams and the waking world takes time and patience. Trust the information that you are integrating into your life. Have faith that your night dreams will guide you. As long as you are in a physical body, there is always more to reveal and more to absorb. This is not a final destination: the journey is the purpose.

A New Perspective: Night and Day

We are accustomed to believing that a new day begins either when we wake up or when the clock turns to midnight. The Jewish faith believes that the day is from sunset to sunset. This is important in respect of night dreams because our dream experiences affect our waking life. If we are having a "good" or "bad" day, most of us can relate that to experiences that have occurred throughout the day (or our waking life). However, as you will see from using the tools in this book, the emotional and mental events on any given day can be a result of dream events.

Given that the quality of our dreams on an individual night can be a major influence on how our day is going to be, it is easy to understand why we might want to change our night dreams upon awakening. Also, since a new day begins at sunset, a great way to start the new day is to set intentions for your dreams, just as you might set your daily intentions.

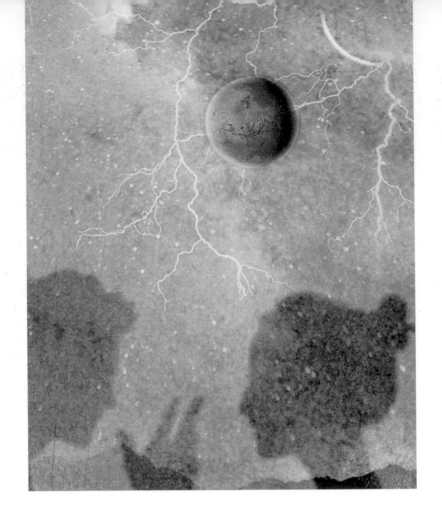

who is who in a dream?
IT'S YOU!

When you dream, you need to understand that everyone and everything in a dream represents qualities of yourself. In your dream, you are the aspect of yourself that you identify with in the waking world, while other people are aspects of your subconscious mind. Your dream is telling you to get in touch with these qualities within yourself.

If there is someone in your dream who you are not particularly fond of, or who has traits that you dislike, remember, that person is an aspect of your own being that (in the present time) you have an aversion to. Conversely, if there is someone in your dream who has qualities and attributes that you admire and wish to emulate, guess what? You already embody those traits, otherwise they would not be coming from within you! Now is the time to integrate and express those traits in your inner and outer world. Don't forget, we are all born with qualities that need to be transformed.

people you don't recognize in a dream

Now, what about the people in your dream who you do not recognize from the waking world? They are elements of your being that are dormant and latent, but still actively a part of your subconscious mind. They are showing you aspects and qualities of yourself that you need to notice and either get in touch with or merge with.

gratitude for those who appear in your dreams

It's important to have gratitude for the people who appear in your dreams, especially those to whom you may have aversions to or those who have qualities to which you have aversions in your waking life. Although you may not want to admit it, these people are the keys to embracing the totality of your being. Why? Because these people came in a dream to share elements of yourself with you.

As a matter of fact, you don't need to wait for a night dream in order to start to show gratitude for those people who you may find it difficult to get along with. Try to find common ground. Be honest. Are the qualities in these folks resonating with qualities that you do not like about yourself? Are they being a mirror for you? If you are not sure, take notice of your actions over the next couple of days and then come back to this question. Remember, according to the principles of mind–body integration, we are all in the process of becoming and working through our life lessons and obstacles.

When I corrected dream images of those to whom I had an aversion in waking life, not only did the dream change, my relationship with that person changed as well. Why? I simply accepted that person's qualities as an aspect of my own being. If you accept the people in your dreams, you are, in turn, accepting who you are.

images in dreams

Just as everyone in a dream is an aspect of the bigger picture of you (see page 36), so images are reflections of your inner world. Although there are many universal images, images come from within the dreamer, and from the dreamer's connection to the "above," which uses people, places, and things to capture the dreamer's attention. Some images will be known to the dreamer, others will need to be uncovered. As we have seen, images are embodiments of emotions, beliefs, experiences, relationships, and even our physical state of health. The types of image and scene we can encounter in our dreams are limitless.

Can you remember any images in your recent or past dreams? If so, write them down in your dream journal (see page 134). Take a few moments to ask yourself what these images mean to you. Sure, there can be many meanings and you may need guidance and support. Be patient with yourself and be careful not to claim with certainty that you know what these images mean or reflect in you. What is certain is that these images came from you. It was a real dream experience.

Below are some examples of images from dreams:
• I am standing on the ocean. To my left, I witness a swirling wind coming toward me, then I look up to the blue sky and am astonished to see a purple sun. To my right, there is a white lifeboat with three pink flags.

- I am walking on the moon and notice a ladder going down to the earth. I know I need to take it, but still it might be scary.

- I am in the house where I grew up. I look at my face and am horrified to see it changing as I get vitiligo (a skin disorder). I run downstairs to my mother and my brother. My mother looks the way she did twenty years ago.

- My father and I are in a red car from 1977. I see that I am approaching the ocean. I yell at my father to put on the brake. I think I am going to go into the water. I am in water. I am on a train with seven people. All of them are strangers but they are all sitting next to one another. I hear the conductor say in a deep voice, "Thank you for riding with us. Final stop: Thirty-Third Street."

Think back to the images you remembered from your recent or past dreams. Ask yourself:

1. How did you feel upon awakening?

2. What was the setting?

3. What was the main drama?

It's possible for all of us to encounter the same images in dreams, and even to have the same dream. Yet as a result of your individual beliefs, experience, culture, religion, and health, your dream will be unique and central to your own life. For example, if five people dream of having coffee in Paris, the same setting and with the same people, each person's dream will have a different meaning.

There can certainly be universal images in dreams, but before consulting a book or asking a friend, why not get in touch with yourself and ask what it means to you? By looking into yourself, you will be one step closer to eventually mastering the self.

As you work through chapter 3 of this book, you will be supported in accepting yourself and moving through your limitations. As you spend more time working with dreams and images, the meanings will come to you much more quickly. Take it one step at a time.

the meaning of numbers, colors, and directionality in dreams

When we dream, we encounter a world that gives information in all manner of ways, including numbers, colors, and directionality. Numbers represent quantities of an image, colors represent qualities of an image, and directionality represents possible courses, avenues, and roads in a dream's directions.

NUMBERS

Dreams often signify an individual's state of mind and whether the mind is in union or in some kind of conflict with the event unfolding in the dream. For example, if you dream of two doors that you need to choose between, or you come to a split in the road, likely this signifies conflict in a decision.

The meanings for numbers one through twenty

ONE   ONENESS, UNITY.

TWO   DIVISION, CONFLICT.

THREE   INTEGRATION, COMING TOGETHER AFTER BEING DIVIDED.

FOUR   DEVELOPMENT, BUILDING, CONSTRUCTION, HOME, MARRIAGE.

FIVE   CREATIVITY, LOVE, SEXUALITY.

SIX   REUNION, HEALTH, CONSTRUCTION AT A HIGHER LEVEL.

SEVEN   AMBIVALENCE, POSSIBILITY OF GROWTH, CONTRACTION, OR DISTRACTION.

EIGHT   AN ISSUE FROM THE PAST THAT IS NOT YET RESOLVED OR INTEGRATED.

NINE   INTEGRATION, COMPLETION. (NINE IS THREE ON A HIGHER LEVEL.)

TEN   PERFECTION IN EVERYDAY LIFE.

ELEVEN   DIVISION, CONFLICT. (ELEVEN IS TWO ON A HIGHER LEVEL.)

TWELVE   WISDOM, DISCERNMENT.

THIRTEEN   COMING TO ONENESS AFTER BEING SEPARATED, GOOD LUCK.

FOURTEEN   CONNECTEDNESS, COMPATIBILITY, KINSHIP WITH OTHER.

FIFTEEN   FULFILLING ALL THE POSSIBILITIES.

SIXTEEN   DEATH, REBIRTH.

SEVENTEEN   DIFFICULTIES FINDING A WAY.

EIGHTEEN   LIFE.

NINETEEN   GRACE.

TWENTY   TROUBLE, DIFFICULTY IN MARRIAGE OR RELATIONSHIP.

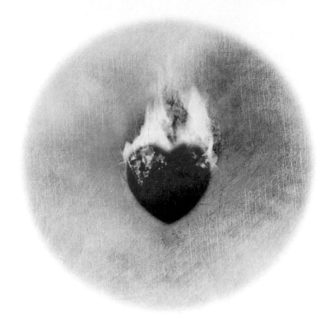

COLORS

Colette Aboulker-Muscat would tell her students that colors are a dream within a dream. Colors in dreams represent emotional and/or physical qualities that need attention. Generally, an excess predominance of one color may mean that there is a physical or emotional issue that needs attention. Also, the lighter and clearer the color, the more immediately the attention is needed.

Many of these color associations manifest themselves in our language. For example, have you ever heard people use expressions such as "he was red with rage," "she was green with envy," or "he had a yellow streak?"

What colors represent

RED   HEART, CARDIOVASCULAR SYSTEM, SEXUAL ENERGY, ANGER, FURY.

YELLOW: URINARY SYSTEM, ENERGY, COWARDICE.

BLUE: THYROID, SPIRITUAL ENERGY.

SKY BLUE   SPIRITUALITY.

PALE BLUE   DETACHMENT.

NAVY   DEEP EMOTIONS.

ORANGE   LIVER, FEMININE STRENGTH, FERTILITY.

GREEN   GALLBLADDER, ENVY, GROWTH.

GREY   BRAIN, REASON, GUILT. (PLEASE CHECK GUILT FIRST.)

VIOLET   EMOTIONAL LIFE.

PURPLE   PRESSURE FROM OTHERS WHO DO NOT UNDERSTAND YOU.

WHITE   LYMPHATIC SYSTEM, PURITY. (AS LONG AS WE ARE ALIVE THERE WILL NEVER BE PURE WHITE OR PURITY. THERE WILL ONLY BE SHADES OF WHITE BECAUSE WE ARE ALWAYS INTEGRATING DIFFERENT ASPECTS OF THE SELF. PURE WHITE IS SEEN ONLY WHEN WE PASS ON.)

DARK BLACK   DEATH. (THIS DOES NOT MEAN DEATH OF LIFE, IT MEANS DEATH OF AN ASPECT OF LIFE. MEETING DREAMS ARE OFTEN IN BLACK.

SHINY BLACK   REBIRTH, LIFE, TRANSCENDENCE.

BROWN   EARTH AND CONNECTEDNESS WITH ALL OTHER COLORS, CONNECTING TO OTHER PEOPLE.

directionality

When reading a dream it is imperative to be aware of where images and people are in the space of your dream. The qualities that are in specific places in your dream determine where you are stuck, where change is difficult, or where change is occurring and possible.

I often ask my clients to draw a picture of where people are in the climacteric (the most important parts) of a dream. These drawings are very useful tools for remembering where people were in a dream.

EXAMPLE OF DIRECTIONALITY IN A DREAM

Let's use a client's dream depicting the inner world of the dreamer as family members as an example of how to read directionality within a dream. At the climacteric of my client's dream, they walked into a room and their family was all there. I asked the client to draw where the family members were in the room:

- The father was in the lower left of the drawing, which shows that the dreamer is ready with issues and challenges.
- Toward the lower right of the drawing was the dreamer's brother. When I asked my client about their brother, the first thing the dreamer said was that the brother just moved to college, which would indicate that there is something that needs to be learned. College education typically lasts four years, so perhaps this suggests a long journey.
- The dreamer's grandfather was in the upper right of the drawing, which indicates that the dreamer aspires to be like their grandfather.
- Directly above the grandfather was the sister. This indicates both future aspiration (upper right) and transcendence (straight above).
- In the upper left of the drawing was the mother. When I asked my client about her, the dreamer said their mother was sneaky, meaning that the dreamer is attached to their own sneakiness.

What the individual directions represent

LEFT	THE PAST.
UPPER LEFT	STUCK IN CHANGE, DIFFICULTY IN TRANSFORMATION, STAGNANT.
LOWER LEFT	SOMETHING IS STARTING, THE BEGINNING OF CHANGE, POTENTIAL, READINESS TO DEAL WITH ISSUES.
RIGHT	THE FUTURE.
UPPER RIGHT	FUTURE ASPIRATION.
LOWER RIGHT	START OF CHANGE.
STRAIGHT ABOVE	TRANSCENDENCE, CHANGE.

chapter 2

your dream toolbox: getting ready to dream

It's time to open up to your imagination and become an active dreamer. Whether you are a first-time dreamworker or an experienced practitioner in search of new tools, this chapter will engage your mind in imagination and teach you how to prepare yourself for dreaming. You will become aware of blockages that can prevent you from recalling dreams, discover how to remember your dreams, learn to use a dream journal, and become accustomed to the best posture when awake for using imagery and changing your dreams.

opening up to the imaginal realm

We all have the ability to use our imaginal realm. As I mentioned in Chapter 1 (see Mental Imagery, page 19), we use our imagination all the time when we think about something. Now we are going to learn how to direct our imagery.

Let's start with a few simple imagery exercises to help you flex the muscles of intention, imagination, and will. Don't worry if you feel or think you are not doing them correctly. It's your imagination and it can flow spontaneously. Trust the process.

imagining three balloons

Your spine is a representation of your personal growth. For this exercise, you need to sit with your spine aligned. This allows the spine to be grounded while ascending to heaven. The ascension of our spine is connected to the vertical axis, as opposed to lying down, when the spine is connected to the horizontal axis and represents our linear world. This seated position also allows your breathing to be deeper and more relaxed. Unless otherwise specified, you will use this position for all the seated exercises in this book.

1. Sit with your spine straight, your feet on the floor, and your hands on your knees. Close your eyes.

2. State your intention to become accustomed to imaginal work. You can say your intention out loud or silently to yourself.

3. Inhale through your nose to the count of six, then exhale through your mouth to the count of eight. Do this three times.

4. In your mind's eye:

• See a bag of assorted balloons.

• Open the bag.

• Notice three balloons.

• Use one hand to remove the three balloons from the bag.

- Look at the three balloons. Notice their colors, texture, shape, and flexibility.

- Take one of the balloons and blow it up. Sense your breath when you breathe into the balloon.

- Feel the texture, size, and flexibility of the inflated balloon.

- Feel free to play with the balloon—tap it up and down.

- When you are ready, let the balloon free.

5. Inhale through your nose, then exhale completely through your mouth. Open your eyes.

How did you do? If you found this exercise difficult, don't worry. Your imagination is like a muscle; you just need to begin to flex it every day. If you found it really difficult, the next two exercises should help.

imagining your morning routine

In this exercise you will start to use your intention and will in the imaginal realm. This is a prelude to what is to come when correcting your dreams. You will see how mental imagery is also about giving your imagination direction and purpose.

1. Sit with your spine straight, your feet on the floor, and your hands on your knees. Close your eyes.

2. Inhale slowly through your nose and then exhale completely through your mouth. Imagine waking up in the morning, getting out of bed, and going through your morning routine.

3. Inhale slowly through your nose and then exhale completely through your mouth. Imagine turning on your smartphone and ask yourself:

• What do you see?

• What was your last message?

• What was your most recent call?

• Which recent images do you remember?

4. Inhale slowly through your nose and then exhale completely through your mouth. Imagine a recent positive event.

5. Open your eyes and smile.

body scan

Scanning the body is a very common practice for discovering stagnation or blockages. This exercise allows you to feel, see, and experience what is happening between your emotional, mental, and physical realms. Have you ever had a massage and thought, "Oh gosh, I did not know I had any discomfort there"? Well, the same holds true for when you scan the body.

1. Sit with your spine straight, your feet on the floor, and your hands on your knees. Close your eyes.

2. Inhale slowly through your nose and then exhale completely through your mouth.

3. Focus on the top of your head. Notice the sensation of bringing your consciousness to this area of your body. Take at least one inhalation and exhalation and then ask yourself:

- Do you notice any tension?
- What does it feel like?
- What does it look like?
- Are there any colors?

3. Repeat step two for each of the following areas of your body in sequence:
- Neck
- Shoulders
- Arms
- Chest
- Abdominal wall
- Abdominal organs/lower abdomen and organs
- Lower back
- Hips and legs
- Groin
- Feet
- Toes

4. Inhale through your nose, then exhale completely through your mouth. Open your eyes.

Once you've completed the body scan, go back to any area of your body where you may have noticed discomfort, any image, or any sensation that you would like to change to initiate a state of wellbeing. The possibilities for change are endless, but here are some examples:
- If you see a knot, you can untie it.
- If you see a glob (a mucus-like ball), you can turn it into a flowing river or a flower. Perhaps a pink flower, a color connected to health.
- If you notice a dark color, change it to a lighter shade or white light.

If you feel overwhelmed, start slowly. If you like, you can pick just one area, image, or sensation to work with. Remember, the microcosm is within the macrocosm: you will be shifting more than this image and it will resonate through your body.

Afterwards, I recommend that you draw a picture of how you transformed the area(s), image(s), or sensation(s) to a state of health and vibrancy. You can keep a record of this drawing in your dream journal (see page 134).

relaxation and becoming receptive

All too often we don't allow ourselves enough time to relax at the end of the day before we move on to the next action we need to perform. This section will give you the tools you need to relax and become receptive to your dream world, honoring it as a reflection of your waking day.

cleansing from the day

This is an exercise that is called "reversing." Events cannot be changed, for they are already in the past, but you can experience the memory and change it to one of your liking. This is a beneficial thing to do at the end of the day before retiring for the evening. Remember, the new day begins at sunset, so the evening is a new day.

Have you ever said something you really regretted or felt dumb or a little embarrassed about afterwards? Well, if you go through the imagery application in this "reversing" exercise, you will find out if those experiences give you the aforementioned sensations. And if they do, guess what? You can transcend what you are embodying and create a positive new sensation.

Remember, in your imagination the situation of the past does not change, but your thoughts and the images of the situation do. And this leads you into living a more positive, centered life with much less looking back into the past. Instead, you can move into the future with kindness.

With practice, you will be able to examine your entire day in reverse and become clear about what worked for you emotionally and mentally, and what did not. A benefit specific to this exercise is that likely it will keep you from suppressing bad experiences and help you to release any feelings of frustration, anger, and resentment.

Let's do the reversing so we can move forward.

1. Sit on a chair with your spine straight. Feel your tailbone on the chair and your feet grounded on the floor. Alternatively, you can lie down on your bed for this exercise.

2. Bring your consciousness to right here and right now. Close your eyes.

3. Inhale through your nose and then exhale completely through your mouth. Do this three times.

4. Now, you are going to start reversing through your day starting from the present moment. Slowly move toward the early evening. Do you notice any situations that you would like to change or any experiences, actions, or interactions you want to shift? If you do, imagine new possibilities for those situations and correct them. Do you notice any uplifting events? If you do, express your gratitude for those events by bringing your consciousness to your heart—this will usually be experienced as a sense of love and warmth.

5. Repeat step four for each of the following times of day in sequence:

• The midpoint of your day

• Late morning

• Morning

6. Knowing that you have corrected and reversed your embodiments of today's events, as well as practiced gratitude for any uplifting events, take a deep breath through your nose, then exhale through your mouth for longer than your inhalation. Smile. If you are seated, begin to feel your feet on the ground and your tailbone on the chair—you are physically grounded in your physical world. Open your eyes and get ready for bed.

a ritual for first-time dreamers

If this is your first time setting up a time to remember your dream or do dreamwork, let's turn it into an initiation into the world of dreams. If possible, try to start dreamwork on the night before a day off work. This will allow you more time to work with the dream in the morning.

About an hour before bed, find a quiet spot in your home where you can be with yourself and be receptive. Know that you are starting a journey that will allow you to experience a different viewpoint, to see in many directions, and at the same time be perfectly present with what is.

Allow yourself the freedom to relax, to breathe, to be present with yourself. Know that you are more than your daytime roles; you came into this world with many purposes beyond your vocation. Part of the "school of life" is to integrate the aspects of the self, heal relationships, take better care of your health and needs, grow into wisdom, and use that wisdom for your daily life. By reading your dreams you are moving toward being self-authoritative and wise.

Remember, this is the start of something new. In order to become proficient, you need to take it slowly but steadily. Below are some more ideas for your initiation into your dream world.

TEAS

Drinking a cup of tea in the evening can help to soothe the nerves, calm the mind, and create a sense of peace, allowing receptivity and openness. Teas can be especially beneficial for those who are new to remembering dreams.

Herbal teas that are particularly suited to relaxation and dreamwork include:

- Mugwort: Known to aid in dream recall.
- Chamomile: Best known as a soothing tea. It may also be beneficial for those who have nightmares.
- Melissa (also known as lemon balm): Used for millennia for improving mood and relaxing the nervous system. Several recent scientific studies have looked into the effects of melissa on memory. It's possible that it may assist those who want to remember dreams more vividly.

ESSENTIAL OILS

Aromatherapy and essential oils can be used to aid in relaxation before retiring to bed. Essential oils that can assist in quieting the mind include lavender, palmarosa, Roman chamomile, geranium, and vetiver. There is a variety of simple and effective ways to use essential oils. They include diffusing the oils, applying them to specific areas of the body (especially acupressure points), and the palm inhalation technique.

a sample blend for diffusion to relax and calm the mind

You will need

electric, mist, or candle diffuser (I prefer the mist diffuser)

3 drops palmarosa oil

2 drops geranium oil

Fill the diffuser with water and add the essential oils. Turn on the diffuser or light the candle, then breathe in and relax.

a sample blend to place on body points

Acupressure points are "energy centers" that can be used as a means of engaging the body's natural healing capability. Our bodies have over 360 acupressure points, and many are beneficial in relaxing the mind. When a healer uses these points, the idea is to use them as a catalyst for healing and open up a specific acupressure channel in the body.

You will need
5-ml blending bottle (or a small bowl)
jojoba oil
3 drops geranium oil
2 drops palmarosa oil
1 drop lavender oil

1. Fill the bottle with jojoba oil, then add the essential oils and shake or stir for a few moments. Alternatively, combine the oils in a small bowl.

2. Put one drop of the oil blend on your thumb or index finger and then place the oil on the Du 24 point (located at the center of the forehead, a little above the hairline), being careful not to let the oil touch your eyes or eyebrows. Gently massage three small circles over the point.

3. Put one drop of the oil blend on your thumb or index finger and then place the oil on the Yintang point (located between the eyebrows, often called the third eye), being careful not to let the oil touch your eyes or eyebrows. Gently massage three small circles over the point.

4. Put two drops of the oil blend on the Pericardium 6 point (located three finger-widths above the wrist on the inner forearm in between the two tendons). Using your thumb or index finger, gently massage the oil down the meridian to the tip of your middle finger.

5. Now use the palm inhalation technique. Put one drop of the oil blend in the palm of your hand. Using your thumb or index finger, gently rub the oil into your palm for a few seconds. Hold your hand, palm facing up, about 4 inches (10 cm) away from your face. Slowly inhale through your nose to the count of six and then exhale completely through your mouth. Repeat three times.

remembering dreams

One of the reasons why we do not remember our dreams is that we have become accustomed to believing that dreams are meaningless. Another possible reason is that there is an aspect of us that is beyond believing: we know that dreams are very meaningful and contain truth, but we are afraid to acknowledge that truth and take action. It takes willpower to admit where we are and where we are going, and it takes commitment to make changes. Unfortunately, for many of us, fear is stronger than courage, and our positive potential is often left underdeveloped. Arguably, this is a cause of frustration and even depression for many people. Why? Because your soul/subconscious is sharing with you the fact that change is possible, but the conscious you is not heeding the message. One of the hopes for this book is to assist you in acknowledging fear and, if necessary, transforming it into courage.

Here's another possible reason for not remembering dreams. Imagine that a young child wakes from a disturbing dream. He runs into his parents' room and his parents immediately try to soothe him by saying that it was just a dream. On the one hand, sure, this seems correct as it will temporarily calm the child's fears and anxiety. Yet on the other hand, it is telling the child that the experience in the dream has no value and was not a real situation. What happens if the child continues to have dreams that leave him in fear? Instead, why not transform the experience into something fun for the child and suggest that he embody a superhero or cartoon character to face the monster?

In order to remember dreams, you need to start to believe and live as if the dreams are messages for you. Wisdom dreams (see page 133) are there for the sole purpose of your overall benefit. As a matter of fact, the act of reading this book is planting seeds to remember a dream—or if not a whole one, then the most meaningful parts of a dream.

upon awakening

We are habituated to forget our dreams upon awakening. Often when we begin to awaken we are crossing the bridge between the world of night dreams and our waking world. It is during this time that many of us are most aware of our night dreams. This is a very precious time. Most often, we simply notice the dream for a moment then go on with our day. It is imperative that we are present for this experience and be with the dream before getting out of bed. Otherwise, we focus on getting ready for the day—getting up, going to the bathroom, making coffee, brushing our teeth, etc.—and in so doing we forget our dream.

When you are starting to work with dreams, it is essential to record the dream as soon as possible (see page 134), writing it in the present tense, and starting to work the dream. As you gain more experience, you will be able to start your day while you keep the dream in mind. I often work with my dreams over my morning coffee.

overcoming fear

Fear, which goes hand in hand with a lack of confidence, is the opposite of courage and love. When we can love who we are, there is nothing to fear. Why? Because love is equated with truth. We are all in the process of becoming, and we all certainly have

fears. The good news is that we can use our fears to create courage and confidence. If someone embodies emotions such as fear or anger, it means they have more potential to experience the opposite: courage and love.

We all experience fear from time to time, perhaps even several different times throughout the day. Quite often our fears and anxieties are about future events, or are the result of an experience that has left us feeling less than our true worth. In order to succeed, grow, and start new endeavors, we all need a sense of courage and confidence.

WHAT IS YOUR IMAGE OF COURAGE?

Before you do the exercises to overcome fear (see below), it's important to take a few moments to prepare.

1. Sit with your spine straight, your feet on the floor, and your hands on your knees. Close your eyes.

2. Slowly inhale through your nose and then exhale completely through your mouth.

3. Using your imagination, visualize a symbol of strength and courage. It could be an animal or it could simply be something in nature that symbolizes and represents courage. Common symbols of strength include lions, kings or queens, and superheroes such as Superman or Superwoman. This is your imagination. Allow it to work for you.

4. Open your eyes and write down what you imagined in your dream journal (see page 134).

exercise to overcome fear (1)

Do this exercise whenever you feel fear or are timid.

1. Sit with your spine straight, your feet on the floor, and your hands on your knees. Close your eyes.

2. Slowly inhale through your nose and then exhale completely through your mouth. Do this three times.

3. Become your symbol of strength (see page 63).

4. See yourself and feel yourself as a symbol of strength walking, commanding, and directing your energy.

5. Open your eyes and begin to live with courage.

exercise to overcome fear (2)

If you like, you can try an expanded version of the previous exercise.

1. Sit with your spine straight, your feet on the floor, and your hands on your knees. Close your eyes.

2. Slowly inhale through your nose and then exhale completely through your mouth. Do this three times.

3. State your intention for transforming fear into courage.

4. Know that in your imagination anything is possible. You can change images, scenes, memories, and experiences to your liking in order to create a blueprint for a new way of living for the days ahead.

5. Imagine yourself in a past event where you felt or experienced being timid or afraid. Begin to see it. Begin to feel it and own it.

6. Know that if you own this specific experience it can be transformed. Know that you can transform it to your liking. When you change this experience you become the hero of the situation.

7. Inhale slowly and then gently exhale through your mouth. Open your eyes and live your day with courage and confidence.

your dream journal

I suggest that you get a new journal to keep a record of your dreams. Ideally the journal should be unlined so that you can draw not only what you've experienced in your dream but also the feelings you noticed, since feelings are part of the experience. Often when a dream is illustrated, it really comes to life, and that allows you to "feel the dream."

Dreams are often trying to tell you to be free of constraints. However, if you are already very creative and are looking to create more structure, or need to build boundaries in your life, try using a lined journal instead. This was the case for me when I started to work with my dreams.

It's a good idea to start your new dream journey with a new "dream pen" or, even better, a few sharpened pencils. With pencils, there is no need to be concerned about ink running out when you're in the middle of writing down a dream. If you would like to add color to your journaling, you can purchase new colored pencils. Another benefit of using pencil is that after you have drawn images or scenes from your dreams that are not to your liking, you can erase them to create new ones. We will get into this

- Dear Subconscious Mind, please inform me about _____ through a dream.

- Dear Higher Self, please inform me about _____ through a dream.

- Dear Soul, allow me to remember my dreams.

- Tonight, I choose to remember a dream.

- Tonight, I choose to connect to my Soul/Subconscious Mind and remember a dream.

- I command my Subconscious Mind to bring forth a dream to remember.

when we discuss changing images in your dreams in order to change the blueprint of the time yet to come (see page 86).

In order to get the most out of your dream sessions, it is imperative that you are honest with yourself and practice self-honesty (see page 29). Our first relationship is with our self, and once we can begin to be honest with ourselves, we can be more truthful in all other relationships. Remember, we are all in the process of becoming. This is a big step in the process of self-realization and becoming the best of yourself, integrating all parts of your being in total wellness.

Honesty is one of the keys for using the imaginal realm. If you start with truth, all else will come into alignment. Let the truth for where you were in life and where you are in life propel you to ascend to greater heights and fulfill your potential. As long as you are here in the physical body, there is always a place to grow and to become.

how to use your journal

Before you go to sleep, write today's date and tomorrow's date in your journal, for example July 18th–July 19th. Why should you do this? Because you go to sleep on the 18th and wake on the 19th. You can also just put the evening's date or the following day's date.

Write down your intention in your dream journal. Take a look at the intentions below. If any of them fit for you, great, use them. If not, know that you can come up with the correct one yourself.

Leave the journal open on your nightstand with your pen or pencil on top of it, ready to record your dreams (this symbolizes being receptive). If there is anything else on your nightstand creating clutter, clear it away to ensure clarity.

While you are relaxing in bed, gently and calmly remind yourself of your intention to dream a dream of meaning.

Honesty is one of the keys for using the imaginal realm. If you start with truth, all else will come into alignment.

your goals in life and your goals in dreamwork

Write down up to three things that you would like in life. Make sure to frame your goals positively—always write what you want in life, not what you don't want. Here are some examples:

- I want to have a better social life or be more sociable.

- I want to start dating.

- I want to find a career that suits me.

- I want to be more connected to myself.

- I want to be financially secure.

- I want a new home.

- I want to travel this year.

- I want to take better care of my body.

- I want to learn to forgive and be happier.

chapter 3

waking from the dream and mining the diamond

In this chapter, you will discover what it takes to be an outstanding and accomplished dreamer. You will be given the practical tools you need to make significant corrections in your dreams, and thereby your waking life too. You will learn which dreams to work with when you remember three or four per night. You will develop a precise and focused way to write down or draw your dreams. You will start to gain clarity about the overview of a dream, and identify any red flags or images that stand out. And you will learn how to correct and/or transform your dreams to guide your life in a healthier direction.

Please remember that this is a journey into the self, which knows where you've come from and where you are, and gives you choices to direct your future. Now is the time to engage with your self with openness and honesty. Sometimes when truth arises, you may not like to see certain aspects of your self, which makes it a perfect time to develop compassion. There is no need to like all aspects of the self; instead, try to rise above the concept of "like" and move into the world of expansive love.

Consider yourself as a diamond in the rough. As with any jewel that is unearthed, it will take time and practice to mine, dust off, and polish the diamond that represents yourself. In order to gain clarity and wisdom you need to search inward, uncovering aspects of yourself and asking—and answering—questions that will help you to discover your wisest, truest self. Are you ready to take the next steps on your journey? Then let us continue.

deciding which dreams to work with

If you remember several dreams upon waking, which one should you engage with? This is a question that comes up a lot in my dream classes. The answer is that the dream you choose to work with is the correct one. Of course, if you have a dream that awakens you in the middle of night, that's the one you should work with. And if you remember only one dream, then the decision is made for you. Trust that the dream you are engaging with is the right one. After all, your soul or subconscious mind already knew which one you would pick. Also, be aware that dream messages come in a variety of forms and images, which means that it is possible, and likely, that the different dreams will all give you the same message.

Here are some questions to ask yourself when deciding which dream to work with:

- Did you wake from the dream?

- Did the dream have an emotional impact on you?

- Did you notice dreams or images that you found to be uncomfortable?

- Which dream experience is the most vivid?

- Which dream involved an experience that you would like to correct?

- Which dream do you feel has the most immediacy?

- Did you wake and say to yourself, "Thank G-d, it was just a dream!"?

Remember that dreams often outline the day ahead, so if you want to have a more positive day, it is a good idea to select an image that evokes emotion or causes uneasiness and then use mental imagery (see page 19) to transform that image into a more positive one. This shouldn't be too difficult, as many of the dreams we remember include images that aren't to our liking. Keep in mind that your soul is trying to grab your attention.

what if I only remember a "blip" of a dream?

Many new dreamworkers are concerned that they didn't really dream, or remembered just one image or a quick "blip" of a dream. If you remember only one image, take this as a positive reinforcement that you are on the right path and trust that the image you received has information for you.

Often when people say they did not dream, what they are really doing is devaluing themselves. This is especially true when new dreamworkers wake for the first time after setting the intention to dream. Like everything else in life, we can only start from where we are, so there is no need to be discouraged. The very act of reading this book has planted seeds to remember a dream, and now those seeds are starting to sprout. Keep allowing the seedlings to grow, and soon you will have plants, and then, eventually, a whole colorful garden of dreams.

Let your dream-maker—your soul/subconscious--be your teacher. Remember, everything you encounter in your dreams is an embodiment and reflection of qualities within yourself (see page 23). Even if you remember only a single image or blip of a dream, you will still be able to work with it to bring meaning into your waking life.

Here are some examples of images or blips that may appear in dreams:

- A sword.

- A falling snowflake.

- A lamp with its light off.

- A small cut on the foot.

- Trying to plug something in, but it won't turn on.

- A lamp with no light.

- A pizza.

- Skiing down a hill.

- Seeing an image of an old friend (or anyone else, for that matter).

- An unpaved road.

- A page in a book.

red flags

Anything that feels out of place in a dream would be considered a red flag. Most often, red flags are the most vivid and alive images in the dream. They are there to grab your attention, so that when you wake up you say, "What was that all about?"

Red flags come to us in a dream as something that is just not right, something that is out of place, or something that is very clear. They often point to the necessity of the dream. In other words, they are there for you to question upon arising, and likely are there for you to transform.

Here are some examples of red flags in dreams:

- I am taking a walk in my favorite park and everything seems normal. When I look up and to the left, I see two trees with gray and yellow withered leaves and decaying orange flowers, yet all the other trees to the right look beautiful and happy, with healthy green leaves and large pink and purple flowers.

- I am getting a massage and the table is slanted because it has only three legs.

- I am driving a car backward.

- I am at home but there is no roof on the house.

- I am wearing clothing that I would not wear in waking life.

working with your chosen dream or image

Many of us do not have time to write down a dream each morning, so here is a valuable exercise to do weekly. Pick one day a week to wake and practice dreamwork, and use your selected dream, image, or red flag from that night for self-exploration throughout the following week, or even up to one month.

You will learn more about how to uncover the main theme of a dream in the next section (see page 81). In the meantime, here are some general ideas to help get you into the self-exploration mindset:

• Don't make anything worse.

• Choose to respond mindfully.

• Create organization in life.

• Have more fun.

• Be more sociable.

• Take time for yourself.

• Start to exercise.

• Start to look for a new job.

• Reconnect with an old friend.

• Remember the goals you made before starting the dreamwork (see page 69).

Dreams are usually one step or more ahead of you, so even if the message does not make logical sense, give it a try.

writing your dream

Now that you have remembered a dream, it is time to open up your dream journal (see page 134) and begin to engage with your dream in the waking world. It is time for you to activate the muscles of your willpower by writing the dream and/or articulating it with drawings.

Writing the dream is essential, especially at the start of dreamwork. Why? Because it connects the imaginal realm (see page 48) with the physical world, which is one of the purposes of working with the imaginal realm. Writing the dream is a seminal step in bridging between the waking world and the dream world. It creates the space to expound the dream, honoring it as a reflection of your waking life and anchoring it in the physical world. As a matter of fact, the emotions you experience and the images you remember as you write the dream, along with the intention to do dreamwork, are the catalysts for bringing the dream into the horizontal reality (see page 12).

Now that you are back in the physical world, you need to follow orderly steps to be successful—you can't build a house without a foundation. I suggest writing the dream from start to end. Doing so may jog your memory and bring forth more dream information. Begin your first sentence with the words "I am" and let the dream flow from there. When jotting down the dream, do so in the present tense. Writing the dream as if it is happening allows you to remember it more easily, and helps feelings and images to come to the surface.

Another option is to draw the dream, or at least its pivotal moments. This will make the dream become more alive, helping you to remember more and experience the feelings that were part of the dream.

what if you wake from a dream in the middle of the night?

It's possible that you may wake from a dream in the middle of the night and want to make a note of it straightaway, rather than waiting until morning. If that's the case, it's okay simply to write down the main events of the dream, and return to it when you are fully awake in the morning.

To help you write down a dream during the night, it's a good idea to use a pen with a built-in light that only illuminates the page where you are writing. This means that you don't have to turn on a lamp to record your dream.

Here are a couple of examples of dreams written down in an abbreviated form:

• I am walking home and end up taking a wrong turn somewhere. I start going down a hill in Park Slope, Brooklyn. I am thinking of asking someone where I am, but then finally see Park Place. As I am walking toward Park Place, I suddenly see rows of green and red vintage cars. I look a little closer and I notice that there is one particular car that is the most prized. It is made of white gold and has three blue stripes. I become very confused. Then I see my best friend and he starts telling me why.

• I am traveling in a place I have never been to before. I know it is in Europe. I am with other people in some kind of tourist group. My high-school friend Michelle is to my right. We are in the middle of an open airbus, and we do not know where we are or where we are going. I am bored and would rather go back to the hotel.

Writing the dream as if it is happening allows you to remember it more easily, and helps feelings and images to come to the surface.

Another option for recording dreams during the night is to use a digital recorder. This may be your best bet, as it is easier than fumbling with a pen and paper in the middle of the night. You can listen to your notes about the dream on the recorder throughout the day if you want more insight.

creating an overview of your dream

Now it is time to read the dream receptively and bring forth information from the dream world into the waking world. This will help you to start seeing the correlations between the two worlds. At first, this may seem like a lot of work, but after some practice it will flow more easily.

Here are the three basic questions you need to ask yourself in order to create an overview of the dream:

1. How do I feel upon awakening? (Your feeling upon awakening shares the present emotion around a waking-life issue, and often indicates your predominant mood and/or feeling for the day ahead.)

2. What is the setting of the dream? (The setting of the dream shares where you are in your inner life.)

3. What is the main drama? (The main drama shares the climactic part of the dream.)

These three questions will lead you to a general understanding of the dream. With practice and honesty, eventually you will be able to create an overview of your dream in under five minutes. Remember, honesty is the key to living in truth.

Using your dream journal, ask yourself these three basic questions and then write down the answers using a single sentence. For example, your overview might be: "I am nervous on a plane heading to Oregon, and there are only ten passengers on the flight."

Next, ask yourself these three follow-up questions:

1. Where in my waking life do I feel this way? (There may be more than one area of your life that you feel this way.)

2. What comes to mind when I think of this situation? (When the situation is a mode of transportation, I often ask clients what it is about that mode of transportation that separates it from the others.)

3. What is the main drama of the dream and what does it remind me of or reflect in my waking life?

For example, if the dream overview was about feeling nervous on a plane heading to Oregon with just ten passengers, you might ask yourself:

- Where in my life am I nervous?

- What does Oregon mean to me?

- What does being somewhere with just a few people remind me of?

taking a deeper look at your dream

When I ask first-time dreamworkers what the setting or an image in the dream means, usually their initial reaction is "I don't know." And my response is, of course, "You know it comes from you!" So let's bypass "I don't know" and fast-forward to "I know what this image or setting means, and let me take a moment to contemplate it." Night dreams provide a vantage point, not from the waking world, but from a place that is aware of your past, present, and future. They come from a place of wisdom, where you can find information on how to proceed in life, all the while knowing it is up to you to make the decisions in your waking life.

Your conscious self may be unaware of the part of you from which your dreams come, so you must expand your awareness, knowing that you can bring the meaning of your dreams to light. Often we are not willing to admit the meaning of an image or a scene because of shame, guilt, or embarrassment. You will need to practice self-honesty. Please be aware that once you admit the meaning of your dreams, you are one step closer to living with emotional freedom, and you will be able to start to

make corrections and changes in the waking world based on information in the dream state. Nothing worth anything is given for free, so if you want the truth from your dreams, you must work for it.

example: reading a dream

Let's use a dialogue I had with one of my clients as an example of how to read a dream receptively.

WRITING THE DREAM

Here are the abbreviated notes my client wrote about the dream:

I am at a Japanese restaurant. There are six ping-pong tables. I catch a ping-pong ball in my right hand and throw it back right away. It goes into someone's mouth. There are people dancing and having fun but I feel ashamed and embarrassed.

THE THREE BASIC QUESTIONS

Me: How do you feel upon awakening?

Dreamer: I feel terrible, ashamed, and scared.

Me: What is the setting of the dream?

Dreamer: A Japanese restaurant with friends.

Me: What is the main drama?

Dreamer: When I throw the ping-pong ball back, it lands in someone's mouth.

THE THREE FOLLOW-UP QUESTIONS

Me: Where in your life do you feel terrible, ashamed, and scared?

Dreamer: Sometimes when I need to speak to my coworkers. I am scared about the health of a family member.

Me: What does the Japanese restaurant mean to you?

Dreamer: It is a place that I go to with my friends for fun.

Me: Can you describe a ping-pong ball? There are many other kinds of ball, including baseballs, basketballs, and beach balls, but the ball in your dream was specifically a ping-pong ball.

Dreamer: It is small, white, and fragile.

Me: Remember, everything in a dream reflects qualities of yourself. Do you relate to the words "small, white, and fragile?"

Dreamer: Yes, in my body and in some of my relationships.

Me: Where in your body?

Dreamer: My left knee.

Me: Can you share anything else about a ping-pong ball?

Dreamer: Yes, my brother and I used to have a lot of fun playing ping-pong together.

Me: Okay, you've mentioned the word "fun" a couple of times. When you think of fun, what comes to mind?

Dreamer: I used to love to dance, but since I hurt my knee I haven't been able to go dancing.

A Word About the Idea of Analyzing Dreams

Throughout this book I have been careful not to use the word "analyze." Dreams are real and happen of their own accord. When we dream, we are not analyzing waking life. When we wake and read the dream receptively, we are not analyzing the dream, we are seeing analogies in waking life. You can always change a dream, no matter how long it has been since the original dream took place.

After this snippet of dialogue, my client and I continued to discuss the dream, including the meaning of the six tables, how those tables were connected to reunion with the self, and how even though the client can't dance for fun anymore, there are other areas of her life she can still enjoy, such as playing ping-pong.

This is a good example of how your dream-maker can connect several disparate ideas to get a message across. Lots of us could have a dream about ping-pong balls, but how many of us would equate a ping-pong ball with fun? And when you think about Japanese restaurants, is "fun" the first word that comes to mind for you?

correcting your dream and changing the day ahead

So far you have learned how to write down your night dreams, extract the essential information to create an overview, and read the dream receptively in order to examine its reflection in your waking life. Now you can start to use the imaginal realm to transform and transcend the images and scenes from your night dreams to direct your waking day.

Just as writing a dream and creating an overview of it takes willpower, so does correcting a dream. This time you will be using your imagination to ascend the vertical axis to the spiritual realm. In this realm, your higher self is connecting to the "you" that you identify with in the conscious waking world. In other words, the "big you" (your higher self) is connected to the "little you" (your physical self), and the "big you" that created the dream can show the "little you" how to transform the dream. Essentially, this is a way to unite your higher self with the self.

As you may recall, imagination is highest in the physical realm and lowest in the spiritual realm. The imaginal realm contains cosmic information from the spiritual realm above it, especially how it pertains to your soul. In order to correct a dream, it is essential that you do so in the physical world, and in the most conducive physical position possible (see page 48). Healing does not happen in a linear way, it works on a vertical axis.

why might you want to correct a dream?

It's best to reflect on dreams upon awakening because this is when they are freshest in our minds, and this is also the most opportune time to change them. As I mentioned in Chapter 1 (see page 38), images are an embodiment of emotions, beliefs, experiences, and other qualities of the self that occupy space in your being. When you wake, ask yourself if you want the energy of your day ahead to contain the images in your dream. If the answer is no, it's possible to correct the images and scenes of your dreams to alter your path in waking life.

On the whole, dreams share information about what is happening in our waking life—whether it is an emotion, event, or relationship issue, for example—around the time of the dream. You could imagine your dream as a camera set on top of a very tall building, allowing it to record in all directions. Generally, dreams are at the epicenter of seventy-two hours (three days) of our experiences. Dreams direct us to the immediacy of something, and seventy-two hours is a guide.

Remember, dreams do not come to us in a linear fashion but in a vertical and expansive way, meaning that they can share information about our past and also what will be in the future. In other words, dreams capture all dimensions. There is a place within your being that has this capability, and it has one desire: to make you whole and guide you toward making the best possible decisions for yourself.

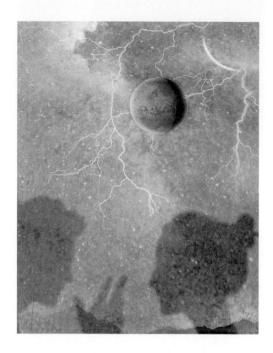

the benefits of correcting a dream

Anxiety and stress can be the result of repressed or unexpressed emotions and feelings. Working with dreams may aid in decreasing anxiety and stress during the day. By going back into a dream and rectifying it, you are not only moving through the anxiety via the imaginal realm, but also creating the space for calmer days ahead.

The practice of correcting dreams offers other benefits, too:

- It can help you to understand yourself—you are your own healer and best teacher.

- It is a creative mental exercise you can use to focus your imagination on bettering yourself, accessing a part of your mind that you have not been paying attention to.

- Recalling and writing dreams is good for the mind and may increase memory function. In fact, journaling by itself is known to be beneficial to the immune system as it decreases stress, perhaps because of the expression of emotions and the meaning of the words used.

The more you practice changing your dreams, the easier it will become, and the more you will experience the union of the waking world and the dream world. You will truly start living as one.

do you need to change all your dreams?

You do not need to change your dreams if you wake up with a sense of contentment. Nor do you need to change a dream in which the experience was positive. In fact, you do not need to change any of your dreams, regardless of your feelings upon awakening. It is up to the individual dreamer to decide if they want to move in the direction of the dream.

The average adult dreams between four and six times per night. With practice, you will likely be able to remember most, if not all, of your dreams. However, unless you have lots of free time and are doing serious inner work, focusing on changing just one dream will allow you enough insight and experience for the day, or even weeks, ahead. The number of dreams you decide to change is up to you. Remember, the same message may come in several dreams; your best bet is to trust yourself and pick a dream.

setting an intention to correct your dream

Before you do the Visualization to Correct the Outcome of a Dream (see page 92), take a few moments to identify the intention you wish to set to correct the dream. The intention should be derived from your overview of the dream (see page 81) and your decision about what needs to be shifted in waking life. If the main theme of the dream is linked to a specific situation, you could include that situation in the phrasing of your intention.

Here are some examples of ways to set your intention to correct a dream:

- If you wake from a dream and feel fear, list three areas in your life where you need more courage. Write your answers in your dream journal, followed by the intention: "I intend to change the dream to one of courage."

- If you wake from the dream and realize that you want to be more sociable in life, ask yourself what are the benefits? What steps could you take to become more sociable? What is one thing you can do this week to be more sociable? Write your answers in your dream journal, followed by the intention: "I intend to change the dream and begin to be more sociable."

- If the theme of the dream was "I make mountains out of mole hills," what are three recent examples of times when you made a big deal out of nothing? Would you act differently if a similar situation came up? Write your answers in your dream journal, followed by the intention: "I intend to change the dream and respond to life calmly and effectively."

- If the theme of the dream is that your life needs more focus, where in your life do you need more organization? List three areas. Write your answers in your dream journal, followed by the intention: "I intend to change the dream to one of order and focus."

- If you wake from the dream and realize that you act immaturely and make situations worse, identify three areas in your life where you have made matters worse or have not acted maturely. Write your answers in your dream journal, followed by the intention: "I intend to change the dream so I can begin to live a life of maturity."

- If the theme of the dream is one of being left out, ask yourself where in your life you are leaving yourself out. List three past or current situations. Write your answers in your dream journal, followed by the intention: "I intend to change the dream and begin to bond with others in my life."

- If the theme of the dream is being disrespected, list three areas in your life where you feel disrespected. Write your answers in your dream journal, followed by the intention: "I intend to change the dream and live a life where I am valued."

- If the theme of the dream is being lost, ask yourself where in your life you need to be found. What is missing in your life? Write your answers in your dream journal, followed by the intention: "I intend to change the dream and live in the waking world with clear direction."

visualization to correct the outcome of a dream

Before you start, you will need to decide on the intention you wish to set to change the dream (see page 89). For this exercise, you need to sit in a position with your spine aligned, which will allow your spine to be grounded while ascending to heaven. You can imagine your vertebrae (the small circular bones that form the spine) as steps on the ladder of growth. As I explained in Chapter 2, the ascension of our spine is connected to the vertical axis—as opposed to lying down, when the spine is connected to the horizontal axis and represents our linear world.

1. Sit with your spine straight, your feet on the floor, and your hands on your knees. Close your eyes.

2. State your intention to change the dream. (For example, "I intend to change the dream to live in courage.")

3. Inhale through your nose to the count of six, then exhale through your mouth to the count of eight. Do this three times.

4. Begin to breathe gently and evenly. Repeat your intention to change the dream.

5. Count down from ten to zero. When you get to zero, see and feel yourself in your mind's eye. See yourself at the climactic part of the dream. Know that anything is possible in your imagination. Use your intention and will to change the images—by doing this you become the authority of your life, ultimately making your inner and outer world more to your liking. (Alternatively, when you get to zero, see a lucid mirror and climb into it, knowing that the dream world is on the other side. Climb into the mirror and find yourself at the part of the dream you would like to correct, or at the climactic part of the dream—your imagination will guide you to the right spot.)

6. Inhale and exhale completely through your mouth. Open your eyes.

Do this exercise every day for at least twenty-one days. If there is anything specific that you have used in the dream to transform it, carry it with you in waking life as a reminder of the personal correction you are making.

example: correcting the outcome of a dream

Let's revisit the example of my client who dreamed about ping-pong balls in a Japanese restaurant (see page 83). This was her original dream:

I am at a Japanese restaurant. There are six ping-pong tables. I catch a ping-pong ball in my right hand and throw it back right away. It goes into someone's mouth. There are people dancing and having fun but I feel ashamed and embarrassed.

After extracting the essential information from the dream and examining its reflection in her waking life, she did the visualization to correct the outcome of a dream, imagining a different ending to the dream. Here is the changed dream:

I am at a Japanese restaurant. There are six ping-pong tables. I am playing ping-pong with my brother, just like we used to do, and we are both laughing. First we play at a small ping-pong table, then we move to a bigger table.

Congratulations on completing this chapter. You have learned to trust yourself to choose which dreams to work with, and if you remember only a snippet of a dream— or even just a single image—you know never to underestimate the value of a "blip" of a dream. You now have the ability to spot red flags in a dream, those out-of-place images that signify something pertinent that needs to grab your attention. You have practiced writing down your dreams and deciphering the correlations between your dream world and your waking life. And, perhaps most importantly, you have learned and experienced changing a dream upon awakening to create a healthier and happier day ahead.

You are now able to dive deeper into your night dreams and bring their analogous meaning into the waking world. If you practice all the lessons you have learned so far with openness, you will be able to achieve a heightened sense of self-awareness and live life closer to your truest self.

chapter 4

challenging dreams

In this chapter we will work with nightmares and recurring dreams, including some possibilities regarding a very popular topic: sexual dreams. As you progress through these pages, you will gain a better understanding of the reflection that such dreams have in your waking life.

In challenging dreams we are quite often getting in touch with our "shadow side." Our shadow side can be thought of as the qualities that we keep within ourselves and do not want to share with others, or as the parts of our psyche of which we are unaware. It can also be thought of as our dark, animalistic side, or as the things we deem to be negative. We can never be whole or truly content until we accept that our shadow side is a part of our being. In other words, in order to become whole, these parts of our psyche need to be accepted. Remember, we do not need to like all the aspects of our being, but we should aim to love and embrace them. Can you embrace who you are and what you are going through? Can you love the totality of your being?

Since dreams carry a wealth of information, they can have many meanings. In this chapter I will allude to possibilities, but please note they are just that—possibilities; they are intended to get you thinking, they are not intended to provide definitive answers.

recurring dreams

Knock knock, it's me again, your recurring dream. Are you going to listen to me this time? Ring ring, hello, is now a good time to talk?

Do you have a recurring dream? Have you ever wondered why you have that dream? We have recurring dreams or a recurring theme in our dreams because we are born with obstacles, tasks, missions to complete, life lessons to be learned, and goals to achieve. Our task is to pay attention to our recurring dreams, be open and honest with ourselves about the challenges we face in life, and use our willpower in the waking world to correct unresolved issues. Remember, our dream-maker always has our best interest in mind.

As I mentioned in Chapter 3, dreams depict where you've come from and where you are presently, and give you choices to direct your future. Even though it is most likely that your dreams are showing you a recurring theme that you are being asked to master, you may also have recurring dreams when a positive shift is happening in your life.

transforming recurring dreams

Generally speaking, recurring dreams often contain "negative" experiences or what I like to call "transformable dreams," because we can transform images that we do not like to our liking.

If you have a recurring dream, you can work with it now. There is no need to wait until you have the dream again. In fact, if you work with the dream now, you won't need to have it again. In other words, you will be freeing yourself to move on to something else. Using your journal, write your dream (see page 77) and use the three basic questions to create an the overview of the dream (see page 81).

Your recurring dream is sharing with you an unresolved issue (or issues) from your past, most often from the first time you had the dream. Ask yourself if there was a similar theme, subject, or experience that was happening in your life at the time you first had the dream. If the answer does not come to you right away, ask yourself to remember the last time you had this dream and reflect on what was occurring around the time of your dream.

The setting of the dream is especially important in recurring dreams because it reflects where you are in your inner life. If you find yourself in the same place in a dream again and again, it means that you are in the same place in your waking world again and again. Ask yourself what was happening during that time of your life.

Once you've examined the recurring dream's reflection in your waking life and decided what issue (or issues) are unresolved, you can use the visualization on page 92 to work with or correct the outcome of the dream.

Once you overcome the obstacle in your life that your night dreams are mirroring, it is likely your recurring dream will have a different, more positive ending. Whether the dream changes during sleep or when you are correcting the dream in waking life does not matter.

common themes for recurring dreams

Each person's dreams are unique, yet we are all part of the same universal consciousness, so many of us encounter similar themes within recurring dreams, and those themes are even more similar for people within the same culture, religion, or social group. Often as we get older, our recurring dreams shift but the themes remain the same.

Common themes for recurring dreams include falling, flying, being chased, being lost, being late for something, drowning, your teeth falling out, being pregnant, sexual intimacy with people who may not be acceptable in waking life, cheating on your partner, your partner cheating on you, being in a classroom, walking into class naked, failing a test, seeing someone who has passed on to the other side, and the end of the world, to name just a few.

The scope of what can be covered in this book is limited, so I decided to review two common recurring dreams in detail: being chased and being in a classroom.

BEING CHASED

If you have a recurring dream about being chased, there is something pressing you need to take a look at in your waking life—after all, everything in a dream is a reflection of your inner world. I have found that people who have dreams about running away from something also have anxiety, often every day. Why? Because those people are avoiding dealing with a specific situation or responsibility. The recurring dream is their soul asking them to deal with it, or to be responsible. They can continue to run away, but the dream will keep coming back with greater intensity, and it is likely that their anxiety will increase in their daily life.

The only way to uncover the situation or responsibility you need to address is to discover what message the chaser has for you. Do you know the person chasing you?

Perhaps if you turn around it will be your best friend or a family member who has your best interest in mind. Or maybe it is someone scary. What is it that causes you fear? How is the chase taking place? A dream of being chased does not necessarily have to be about running away on foot; it could involve forms of transportation, such as a car, a bus, a bike, or even a snow mobile.

The colors and setting of the dream will help you examine its reflection in your waking life. For example, if there are seven gray cars chasing you while you are riding a bike, perhaps there is guilt that you need to rectify—gray can represent guilt, and the number seven can signify the possibility of growth or contraction (see page 41). And if you are running away from a red bear, perhaps this signifies anger that needs to be felt or seen in the waking life—after all, red is the color of anger and fury (see page 43).

BEING IN A CLASSROOM

The classroom is a common setting for a recurring dream. The setting is of the utmost importance here. What type of classroom or school appears in your dream? Your answer will share what needs to be addressed. The type of classroom or school often indicates your maturity level within this situation. For many of us, if we are sitting in a classroom, we are there to learn something new, so ask yourself where you are in a place of learning. For example, if the dream takes place in elementary school, perhaps you are just starting to learn something new. What does being in school mean to you?

When you wake from a classroom dream, ask yourself the following questions:

- How do I feel upon wakening?

- Do you feel fear? If so, think of three areas in your life where you need more courage. Write your answers in your dream journal, followed by the intention: "I intend to change the dream to one of courage."

- What was it like to be in class when I was this age? Perhaps there is a lesson to be learned from the past.

- Are you currently in a place of learning? (A place of learning need not be a physical location; it could also be a state of mind or a shift in attitude. For example, you may have set the intention to learn how to be more sociable, to be more compassionate, or to study something new.)

- Are you in a new relationship? Or have you just started to learn something new? Often people have dreams about being in class when something new is occurring in their life.

- What has recently been happening in your life?

- Have you been behaving in an age-appropriate manner? If not, was your behavior age-appropriate to the class or school in your dream?

- Did you recognize any of the other students in the dream? If so, which qualities come to mind when you think of those people? Remember, those people are in your dream in order to bring their qualities to your conscious mind.

- Was the school in your dream new or old? If it was an old school, perhaps it represents an old pattern that is playing out. If it was a new school, perhaps you are learning something new.

- Was it a school you recognize?

- What was the lecture the teacher was giving? That can be a big clue. Why? Because there is a teacher inside of you!

- Where were you sitting in the classroom? At the front of the class? At the back? On the left or right? (See page 45 for details about what directionality can represent in dreams.)

Please note that the questions above are not in any specific order, but aimed to open you to possibilities.

Recurring dreams in a classroom often feature taking tests. Here are a few extra questions to ask yourself if your dream included taking a test:

- Do you feel you are being scrutinized in your life?

- Where in your life are you being tested? Think metaphorically. Are you being tested at work or in a relationship?

- Have you been examining your life to a fault?

- Did you pass or fail the test?

- Where in your life can you do better? In your observation, where in your life do you feel you have been failing?

- Is there something that you need to prepare for?

- Where in your life do you feel prepared or unprepared for something?

- What was the subject of the test? Is it a subject that you are familiar with in waking life?

- What can you do in your life to achieve a passing grade? (Be easy with yourself.)

Since night dreams share with us the immediacy of seventy-two hours around the time of the dream (see page 87), your dream may be preparing you for a life test that is coming your way.

more common themes of recurring dreams

Are you running away from an aspect of yourself? Are you trying to evade a responsibility? Are you starting a new endeavor? Has something new come into your life that needs your care and nourishment? Are you living within your value system? Below are a few more common themes of recurring dreams that deal with these issues. As before, the meanings are only examples; it is up to you to decide whether they ring true for you.

PREGNANCY

It's common for women to dream about pregnancy. Often this is sharing with the dreamer that there is something new on the horizon, such as a new part of their personality that they are going to discover or the start of a new endeavor. Men may not have dreams about being pregnant but they can have dreams about having babies or small children, which can be a reflection of something in their life that needs to be nurtured and cared for. For couples, a dream about pregnancy is often precognitive (see page 133).

SEXUAL DREAMS

Many people find dreams about sex to be challenging. This is because sex is connected to so many different parts of ourselves. What is the symbolism of sex in a dream? Sex is a bonding, an intimate union, a coming together between two beings, or two sets of consciousness. However, a dream about sex does not necessarily reflect physical intimacy in the waking world. Instead, it could be about merging with someone emotionally, connecting with them on a deeper level, or it could be about merging the conscious qualities of the dreamer with the qualities of the other person in

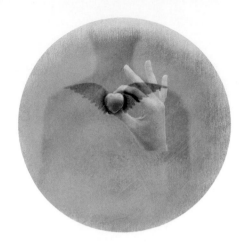

the dream. Is there some thing or some quality that you are becoming close with in your life?

Common sexual dreams include sex with someone famous, sex with an ex-partner, sex with a teacher, and cheating on your partner. Does this mean that you desire these experiences in the waking world? Perhaps, but there is certainly a more enveloping way to look at this. Remember, dreams are a reflection of your waking world, so sexual intimacy with others often means that there is an aspect of that person that you are merging with or integrating within yourself.

Sexuality is intimately tied in with spirituality. Mystics often write about their relation with the divine as if it were a relationship between themselves and their beloved. As Jeremy Taylor, author of *Dream Work: Techniques for Discovering the Creative Power in Dreams*, states, "Over and over again the mystical writers of all religious traditions couch their descriptions of transcendent experience in sexual terms, giving shape to their encounter with the divine as a metaphoric encounter with the 'Lover.'"

cheating

Have you dreamt about having sex with someone who is not your partner? Okay, this is a theme that I hear often during dream sessions. Remember, a dream is an aspect of yourself. When you are having a dream about having sex with another person, you are not necessarily cheating on your partner, you are cheating on an aspect of yourself that your dream partner is reflecting in you. If you are aware in your dream that you are married and cheating, then perhaps there is some area of your life where you are going against your values.

If you wake from a dream about cheating, ask yourself the following questions:

- Is there anything in your life that you are cheating in?

- Where in your life are you being deceptive? (This may not be about deceiving someone else. Perhaps you are deceiving yourself.)

- Where in your waking world have you not been honest?

- Where in your life do you feel insecure?

- What are you doing having sex with this person in your dream?

intimacy with people in a position of authority

Another common sexual dream is one where you are intimate with someone in a position of authority, such as a teacher. What is the role of a teacher? A teacher is there to facilitate learning and can be a symbol of inspiration, wisdom, and experience, so perhaps sexual encounters with authority figures signify that something new is being born inside of you? Existence arises from merging sexually.

Of course, all the possible meanings suggested above are simplistic. It is up to you, the dreamer, to use the tools you have learned thus far (considering the setting of the

dream, colors, numbers, etc.) to understand the reflection of your dream. Next time you have a sexual dream, use the three basic questions to create an overview of it (see page 81)—you may be surprised at what it is a reflection of.

nightmares

The only way out of a nightmare is through.

It is a cold, dark, dreary night. You are walking. You look down and you realize that you are not wearing any shoes. It's very foggy and you feel as if somebody's watching you, but when you look back there's no one there. You start to shiver as the air becomes colder and colder. You feel that somebody's lurking right behind you, but there is nobody behind you. You walk further and you start to feel a new sense that somebody's close by. You look all around but nobody is there. It's getting colder and colder. You feel the cold on your skin and on your feet. You look around to see if anybody is there. You know somebody is there. You just can't see them. You look back and then when you look straight ahead. Aaargh! A disfigured being is staring straight at you. It is holding a knife. You jolt awake with your heart pounding.

It's a beautiful day. The weather is perfect. You're enjoying the beach, watching your children play. Then all of a sudden to the right you see a volcano and you hear loud thunder. The day becomes darker. You feel anxious and scared because you know something terrifying is about to happen. All of a sudden you see lava erupt from the volcano. Oh no! You see everyone running away. You are also running. You look behind you and you can't see your children. You wake up. Your heart is racing and a bead of sweat is coming down your brow.

You are a soldier in battle. You see an army approaching straight ahead. You look to the right and you see a wounded soldier with his left arm blown off. He looks you in the eye. You know by that look that he needs help, so you find your way to him. You look up and see the enemy's airplane right above you. You wake up. You're terrified by this experience. Soon you realize it was just a dream. You take slow breaths, trying, with difficulty, to fall back to sleep... It's not always like this when you wake from a nightmare, but you get the picture. In short, a nightmare is a distressing dream that wakes you up.

Here are some examples of common scenes from nightmares:

• Being chased by a monster.

• Being berated by someone who in real life seems more powerful.

• Being in a dark alley.

• Being chased.

• Your teeth falling out.

• Drowning.

- Crashing into a river.

- A house fire.

- A falling building.

- War.

- Feeling trapped in a maze, a cave, or a house.

- A plane crash.

- The end of the world.

Studies have shown that men have more nightmares with imagery of violence and natural disasters, such as earthquakes or fires. Men are generally alone in nightmares, while women tend to be with friends. Researchers have found that women tend to have nightmares that are more connected to personal relationships, such as a fight with parents, in-laws, or a spouse.

what are nightmares?

There is no such thing as a bad dream. Nightmares wake you because there is something that needs your immediate attention. They come as "bad," negative, or startling dreams in order to alert you. It is almost as though someone in your waking life is trying to share something of importance over and over and over again. Finally, they end up yelling at you and ask if you are even listening. In the case of nightmares, it is your dream-maker (your soul/subconscious) who is grabbing your attention. Your dream-maker is your best friend. A true friend shares the truth with you, and there is no truer friend than your soul/subconscious. Since the point of a nightmare is to wake you up in order to address something immediately, ask yourself what in your life you need to do that you have not done.

   Dreams are often sharing with you what has happened before the dream. This can be especially true with nightmares, because research shows that they are more likely to occur when a person has recently experienced stress and/or anxiety, is prone to anxiety, or has unresolved experiences related to trauma.

Night Terrors

Night terrors are not the same as nightmares. Also known as sleep terrors, they are most commonly seen in young children and resolve during the teen years. However, people of all ages can have them, although they become rarer as we get older. Night terrors can be as short as a minute or last up to 40 minutes, but they commonly last between 30 seconds and 3 minutes.

During night terrors, the dreamer often screams and yells with fear, arms thrashing wildly, and may even stare wide-eyed. Often there is no response when someone tries to wake them out of the terror. Most commonly, the dreamer will fall back to sleep and not remember the event upon awakening.

Night terrors occur in the first few hours of sleep, while nightmares commonly occur in the later parts of sleep. According to the American Academy of Family Physicians, night terrors in adults may be a result of post-traumatic stress, anxiety, bipolar disorder, medication, or drug use.

In contrast, nightmares happen to people of all ages. The dreamer will wake up with an awareness of their surroundings, often feeling panicked and scared, and they will remember the nightmare.

A Word of Caution

Please note that nothing in this section is meant to cure or prevent nightmares. This book is intended for informative and self-discovery purposes. I am well aware that many people have experienced or witnessed trauma, abuse, and other seemingly horrific situations. Nothing can change those experiences, but perhaps if you do have nightmares about such events, you can try changing the images upon awakening, creating a space for calm and healing. I have known people who have been in wars, and just speaking about their dreams helped them to move forward with more freedom.

Gerald Epstein calls nightmares "inner post-traumatic stress disturbances," and believes they are related to post-traumatic stress disorder (PTSD) or traumas that are met in the everyday life. A nightmare (or internal trauma) usually represents a recurring theme from your life, often something that you have been unable to master. Those with PTSD are more likely to have dreams exactly as their memory recalls the event, a true embodiment of the experience. We cannot change the seminal event that caused the initial trauma to express itself, so when we remember a negative yet transformable event, what we are actually doing is remembering the last time we remembered it!

Nightmares can also come as forewarning of an event or unresolved issue that may come up soon. Like other dreams, nightmares can share events from seventy-two hours around the time of the dream (see page 87).

transforming nightmares

I think we can all agree that we wouldn't label nightmares as a "good" experience. But as much as they can be scary and horrifying, they still come to us as a blessing in disguise. They reveal the blockages and obstacles that we need to overcome so that we can live life with more freedom.

Nightmares tend to be clear and vivid, often depicting fear, horror, and anxiety. They can seem very real—and they are. When we are dreaming, our physical body is not aware that we are dreaming, which is why we may be sweating and/or experience palpitations and anxiety when we wake. Often, our first thought upon waking from a nightmare is "Thank G-d, it was just a dream!" Well, that's not quite true. It certainly was not just a dream. The nightmare was sharing with you aspects of your past and present and possibilities for the future that must be confronted immediately. Remember, our waking world and dream world are mirrors of each other.

While the reasons behind nightmares are many, and it may be scary to write down the dream, it is imperative to go through the steps of changing the dream to your liking so that you can become the hero of the dream. As I mentioned earlier in the book (see page 60), if a child has a nightmare it is a good idea to suggest that they embody a superhero (or another symbol of strength) to face the monster and change the nightmare.

Do you want your nightmare to bear more fruit in the waking world? No, of course you don't! Change the dream (see pages 86–94). Do it now.

In order to disown something, first you need to own it, instead of stuffing it down. Therefore, when you go through the steps of correcting the dream it is likely that you will encounter the same or similar emotions to the ones you experienced during the nightmare. These feelings and sensations are likely to arise while you are writing or drawing the dream. Once you have discovered the meaning of the dream, corrected it, and created a new blueprint, it is likely the feelings associated with the dream will no longer be present.

negative self-talk

As the saying goes, you are your own worst enemy. However, you can also be your own best friend. Be mindful of how you speak to yourself. Why? Because the way we speak to ourselves plants the seeds for how our thoughts and beliefs form. For example, if you have a dream where you are yelling at an innocent young child or you

are being yelled at, upon awakening you may say to yourself, "Oh my G–d, I am not an abuser." No, you may not be an abuser of children, or yourself, but how have you been speaking to yourself? If you abuse yourself in the waking life, what do you think will happen in your dreams? Love yourself.

You come from love. During your journey here on Earth, each experience has been designed for you to embody love and to bring to the waking world what you really are. G-d created us in its image so we must be merciful and compassionate.

exercise for easy dreaming

Nightmares depict what is of immediate necessity, but this does not mean we need to experience them regularly. Since dreams are analogous to our waking life, let's see if we can have information passed on in a way that is not a nightmare. In order to do this, we need to become open to the messages in the dream, so the dream does not yell at us!

This exercise uses affirmations that may be beneficial for those who have ongoing disturbing dreams. The purpose of the exercise is to set the intention for promoting and calming the mind before falling asleep.

1. Sit on the side of your bed with your spine straight and your feet flat. Alternatively, you can lie down on the bed or sit in a chair.

2. Inhale through your nose to the count of six, then exhale through your mouth to the count of eight. Do this three times.

3. Begin to breathe gently and evenly. State one of the following affirmations:

All that is in the past can stay there. I open myself up to living with calm, faith, and deep relaxation. I know and allow the Universe/G-d to support me. I intend to listen to any messages in my dream.

I ask my soul/subconscious to provide information for the present time with ease. With each slow breath I take, I can relax more and more and unite my conscious mind with my soul.

I allow myself to rest calmly this evening. With each slow inhalation and exhalation, my body relaxes more and more. With each exhalation, and with each inhalation, I can relax deeper and deeper.

4. Inhale and exhale through your nose.

chapter 5

waking life as a dream

What if you could apply the tools and foundations of dreamwork to your waking day? In this final exploratory chapter you will learn to see waking life as a dream, or a reflection of your dreams. By practicing some of the dreamwork techniques you have learned in this book, you will be able to respond appropriately to your life circumstances, engage with others from the vantage point of knowing that they reflect qualities of your inner world, witness more synchronicities in waking life, and use imagery to live with freedom, security, and overall wellbeing.

your inner waking world

At the start of the book I introduced you to the concept that the dream world and our waking world are parallel worlds and mirrors of each other. Perhaps by now you have experienced the synchronicities and parallels between the waking world and the dream world. Now it's time to use the " integration and dreamwork tools you have learned to engage more intimately with the vertical reality during waking hours. If you do this, it's possible you may experience more pleasurable night dreams.

In mind–body work your present and future are not predicted by your past. The way you acted and felt yesterday does not need to be the way you act and feel today. If you are aware of your tendencies—you know, the kind of thing where you tell others, "Oh, this is just the way I am"—but know deep down inside that it does not have to be that way, then, just as in a dream, you can change those tendencies.

When you live your waking life as a dream, you have the opportunity to correct your day before your dreams. Do you want to relive your day in your dreams? Or would you prefer to rectify your day and clear any issues before you go to sleep, so that you can receive fresh information in your dreams?

As your awareness expands from practicing dreamwork, it will naturally blend into the waking world. Although this book is focused on dreamwork, the goal is for you to live a full, spiritual life, embracing all that you are and embodying love for all your qualities—both those you are at peace with and those you're in conflict with. The key word here is "love," not "like." Liking something is bound by your personality and ego, whereas love is transcendent. When we can ascend and love our being in totality, the veils of this world become thinner and more permeable and we can start to view life through a lens that is more expansive and all-encompassing.

Just as when you started working with night dreams, pick a day a week to explore your inner waking world. It may be a stretch to think of your waking life as a dream, but try it for a day. Think about it—or better yet, live it as if your thoughts, beliefs, experiences, and interactions are there for you to learn about yourself. Embrace your being with totality and make corrections, if desired, that come from "above" or the invisible reality.

understanding your inner waking world

One of the most practical ways to explore your inner waking world is to see everyone you come into contact with as an aspect of yourself. You may not act in the same way as these people, but you will have similar tendencies. We are all human, so we all have similar tendencies to a greater or lesser extent. After all, if we all come from the same Creator, we must all be connected.

All relationships expose inherent, latent, or already conscious aspects or qualities of your self. Ask yourself:

• Which qualities do the people in your life reflect in you?

• What qualities do they bring out in you?

Accepting these aspects or qualities will allow you to live a life of understanding, compassion, and love. After all, it is yourself that you are being loving toward.

All of us have situations and relationships that we do not sync with completely. Practicing acceptance will allow you to live a more peaceful and loving existence. Sure, this may be a stretch for some people, but try it out for a day.

If you are not ready for this belief, take a look back at your day. In which situations or relationships did you find yourself being content? In which situations or relationships did you feel a sense of discontentedness or negativity? (Actually, let's replace the word "negativity" with the term "transformative emotions.") Do you find yourself stepping back and yielding when you could be more straightforward with others? Do you find yourself being too aggressive in certain situations? Just as our lungs expand and contract with the inhalation and exhalation of each breath, so in life we can expand or contract ourselves in different situations. You need to decide in which direction you are going to move.

We exist in the physical realm, which means that we are bound by time and space. The same does not apply to the imagery we experience in our dreams. You may dream that you are the physical gunslinger or a princess in your waking life, yet you are not that gunslinger or princess. You are not going to bite on your favorite sandwich and have all your teeth fall out. Nor are you going to show up for class naked, see a tornado zip through NYC, or win the lottery—probably! Yet there may be times when you feel as embarrassed as if you had showed up for class naked or as if your heart is a hurricane of spinning emotions.

When you change images in a dream, you are creating a new path to take in life. Remember, images are the embodiment of your emotions, experiences, and beliefs. Therefore, your experience is mirroring back to you the way you behave and react in certain situations, as well as what you are attracting into your life.

When you practice living your waking life as a dream, you need to be mindful, noticing anything that stands out. Have you seen anything in your life that seems out of place or is out of the ordinary? Just as in your dreams, your soul/subconscious is working to give you clues in your waking life. For example, perhaps you look up to the right and notice the same number a few times in a day; or maybe you see specific colors during a day. Once you start living your waking life as a dream, you may come to see that the numbers you notice most during the day have meaning for current life situations or questions you may have. What at first seems random is actually synchronicity. Do you need to take action?

changing the "dream" of daily life

Belief creates our experience, and our experiences are a reflection of our beliefs and what needs to be seen for growth. In the first part of the book you were asked to take a look at some of your experiences and see what beliefs could be attributed to them (see page 14). Now that you have all the tools needed for dreamwork, you can, if you choose, change the "dream" of daily life. For example, if you have an experience of being embarrassed, you can use all the tools of imagination to change the experience, just like when you change a dream upon awakening (see page 86).

It can be a good idea to check in with yourself every three hours to review your experiences throughout your day. Ask yourself whether those experiences enhanced and nourished your life or sucked out your energy and left you feeling depleted? If necessary, you can use the tools you have learned to change those experiences. If you do this, shortly you will notice that your life changes for the better. Remember, you cannot change the past experience itself, but you can change your memory of that event. In doing so, you are using the past experience to propel your self-growth.

Be mindful. Ask yourself whether you are reacting impulsively to the events of the day or responding with clarity and wisdom. There is a difference between a response and a reaction. Most often, you will find that you are reacting—meaning that your action was not thought out, and is likely an impulsive habit. Sure, we need to use emotions to make decisions, but they should not be our only source of motivation. Reactions are propagated by subconscious beliefs. In other words, reactions are the aspects of the self where people say, "Oh, that's just the way I am." Well, is the way you are really the best version of you?

A response, on the other hand, is often calm, thoughtful, and deliberate. Considering the

difference between the short- and long-term results of an action before acting is a quality of responding.

changing your experience of daily life

You are now ready to put everything you have learned into practice. In time it will come naturally to you. Pick one day per week to practice changing the dream of daily life. Check in with yourself a few times per day—for example, at 11 a.m., 3 p.m., and 5 p.m.— or choose to do this at a set time each day, such as during your lunch break.

Ask yourself the following questions:

• How do you feel?

• What is the setting of your experience? (It's easier to define the setting for an experience in waking life because you know where you are!)

• What is the main drama?

• What belief can you attribute to this experience?

• What belief would create a new experience?

Then change the memory so that you can have a new experience.

continuing your journey into the self

Thank you for taking the time to read this book and explore the exercises within it. I hope the time you have spent with your inner self has led you to discoveries that you can bring forth in your daily life and in your relationships. If you take just one thing away from this book, I hope it is the knowledge that we all come from the same Creator, we are all in the process of becoming, and through each thought and action we create.

By using the tools in this book, you can anchor yourself with your deepest purpose, so that you can direct your life to your choosing, overcoming obstacles and challenges along the way. Know that you can overcome any challenges you meet. Think of those challenges as a vital part of your journey: you start out in life as a rough (or unpolished) diamond, and the challenges and obstacles that you encounter gradually polish that rough diamond until it becomes a clear and beautiful precious stone. In other words, the challenges you move through in life all contribute to your growth, until you are able to live life with clarity, truth, and authenticity.

Congratulations on your recent inner work. I encourage you to continue seeking out truth and awareness—not only for yourself, but also for the healing of the world.

types of dream

In this book my focus is on "wisdom dreams," although there are various types of dream that you may also be interested to explore.

COLLECTIVE DREAMING

We are all connected and belong to one consciousness, so it's not uncommon for people to dream about similar things or dream for someone else. This can be particularly true for participants in a dream class, as it causes the members of the class to form a close-knit vessel of consciousness and healing. For a week in my dream class, we set aside one night to dream for someone else in the group. Participants were amazed at how similar their dream experiences and images were. Also, when there are major world events, it is common that they will be a mirror of waking life. Just like in a dream, everything in the waking world is a reflection of the individual.

DREAMWORK

Many ancient cultures and faiths, including the ancient Egyptians, Mesopotamians, Native Americans, Australian aborigines, Hebrews, Christians, Arabs, and Malaysians, believed that night dreams were messages from the invisible reality to be used in waking life. The ancient Egyptians were aware that when we dream our eyes are open, meaning we have greater awareness in dreams. As a matter of fact, the ancient Egyptian word for dream, *rswt*, is connected to the root *ris*, meaning "to be awake." The ancient Egyptians believed that dreams prophesied warnings and guided the dreamer. Pharaohs often called on priests or dream interpreters to make political decisions, and even believed that dreams could connect the living to the deceased. One need only look at the story of Joseph interpreting Pharaoh's dreams in the Torah portion Miketz. Joseph not only interpreted dreams but also experienced prophetic dreams. The Talmud, a book of study for rabbis, states that "nothing happens to a man, good or ill, before he has beheld some intimation of it in a dream." (Berachot section 55a.)

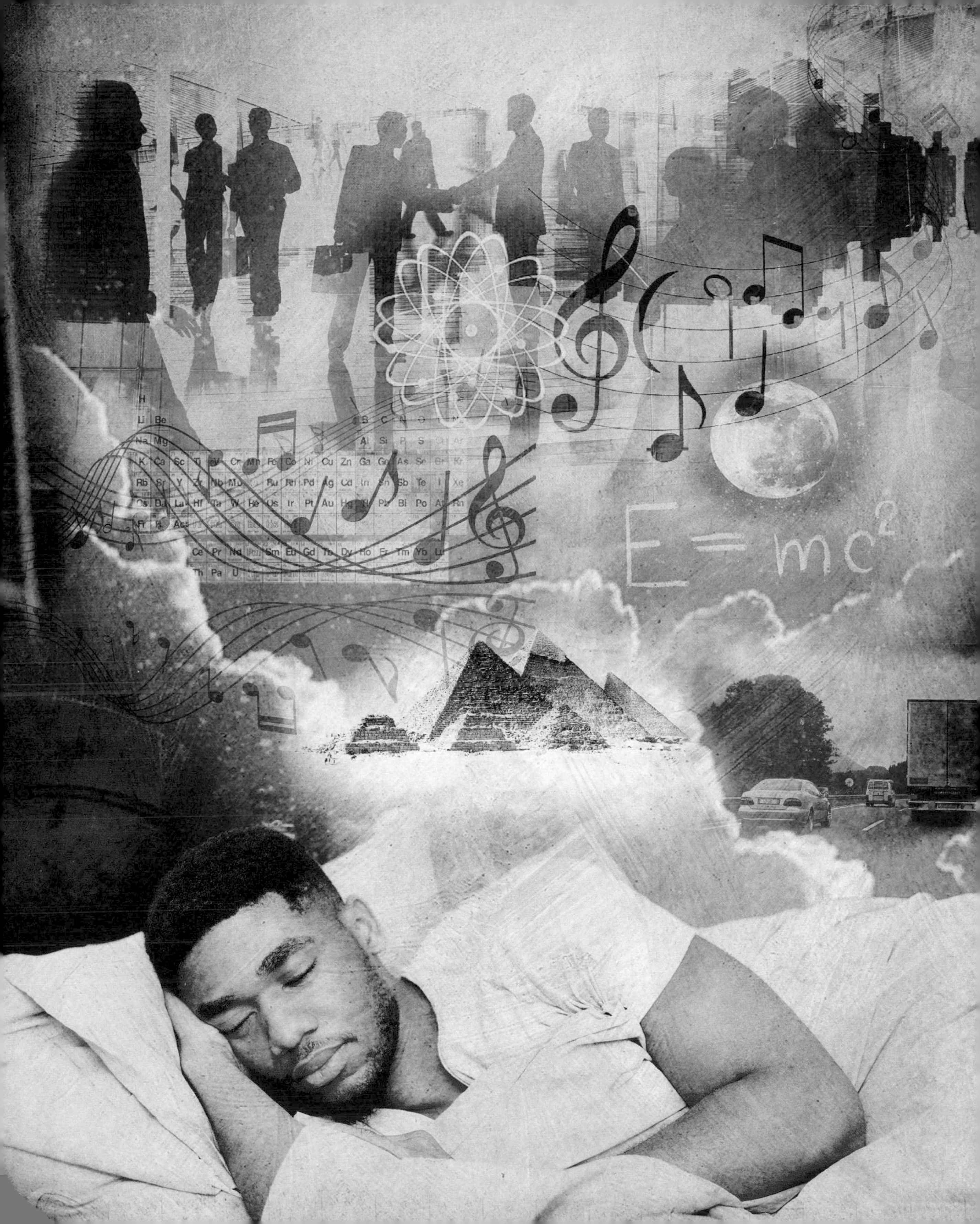
$E = mc^2$

HISTORICAL DREAMS

Dreams have played a significant role in changing the course of history, as is evident in scientific discoveries, musical masterpieces, and even assassinations. In some cases, history has been made because the dreamer did not listen to or work with the dreams. Notable examples include Einstein's theory of relativity, Abraham Lincoln dreaming of his death, the Beatles song "Yesterday," the invention of the sewing machine, and novels such as Mary Shelley's *Frankenstein*. Harriet Tubman used her visions during naps to help see the best way to direct operations for her underground railroad, bringing slaves to freedom.

INTUITIVE DREAMS

These are often the dreams that we have when we wake with an idea or the conclusion to something that we have been working on for some time. For example, Dmitri Mendeleev, the creator of the periodic table, was working on a way to organize the elements of nature. He recalled, "I saw in a dream a table where all the elements fell into place as required. Awakening, I immediately wrote it down on a piece of paper." Like meeting dreams (see opposite), intuitive dreams usually do not speak in story form as wisdom dreams do, but come as a clear message.

LUCID DREAMING

One of the most common questions I'm asked when I teach a class or have a new dream student is: Do I teach lucid dreaming? Lucid dreaming is when the dreamer is aware of dreaming and can act wilfully in the dream, while staying fully asleep. Although people often think of this as having a greater sense of spiritual awareness, I do not think this should be the goal of dreaming. A main aim for dreaming is to see the dream world and waking world as mirror realities. Lucid dreaming will, however, be a natural growth response to the techniques outlined in this book.

MEETING DREAMS

Most often, these dreams are experienced when someone has passed on and there is a direct message from the other side regarding decisions in waking life. In these dreams there is no imagery symbolism. For example: A grandmother came to Jennifer and told her that her aunt was sick and needed to change her medication. Jennifer waited several months before telling her father because she was scared to give the dream any meaning. It turns out that her dream was true. Her father told her that her aunt had changed her doctor and medication and became healthier. Often new dream students share the fact that a deceased friend or family member came to them in a dream. This might seem to be a meeting dream, but it is actually a wisdom dream about the dreamer with the deceased person as an aspect of themselves. Once this is understood, it brings the attention inward to self-discovery.

PRECOGNITIVE DREAMS

This type of dream shares information/knowledge as it comes to fruition. The coming of fruition does not need to be in the immediate future. For example, I know of someone who had a dream in his twenties that he was driving down a highway and a truck smashed into him. Twenty-five years later, he was driving down the road he had dreamt about and he immediately remembered the dream and slowed down. Sure enough, the same truck passed him!

PROPHETIC DREAMS

Prophetic dreams occurred when there were still prophets on the earth. There are many examples of prophetic dreams in the Bible. Prophets were used as channels for G-d. G-d endowed certain people with the gift of vision for warnings and instructions, and to share G-d's plan.

WISDOM DREAMS

These are the dreams that embody our past, our present, and possibilities for our future. They are a powerful tool for self-discovery and personal transcendence, allowing us to access the part of ourselves that has access to the whole of ourselves. Wisdom dreams are there for the sole purpose of your overall benefit.

your dream journal

_____

_____

_____

_____

_____

_____

_____

_____

_____

_____

_____

_____

_____

_____

_____

_____

_____

_____

_____

_____

_____

_____

_____

_____

_____

_____

Index

Further reading

Aboulker-Muscat, C., *Alone with the One,* (ACMI Press, 1995)

Epstein, G., *Healing Visualizations: Creating Health through Imagery* (Bantam, 1989)

Epstein, G., *Healing into Immortality: A New Spiritual Medicine of Healing Stories and Imagery,* (ACMI Press, 2010)

Reznik, P.S., *Face Reading Secrets for Successful Relationships: A Guidebook to Understanding Yourself and Others* (Pomni Publishing, 2016)

Picture credits

Shutterstock: p1, Kamenetskiy Konstantin; p2, p129, Prostock-stuido/Rawpixel.com; p4, Dudarev Mikhail; p5, Woottisak; p8, Mike Pellinni/asharkyu; p23, Aaron Amat; p31, Kate_Koreneva; p32, Woottisak; p46, Mangostar; p50, Dudarev Mikhail; p61, Dima Sidelnikov; p93 Kamenetskiy Konstantin; p96 Thep Urai/wavebreakmedia; p101, SFIO CRACHO; p102, Iakov Filimonov; p109, Chones; p118, GOLFX/Shaiith/aimful; p116 Kate_Koreneva; p123, Woottisak; p129, Prostock-stuido/Rawpixel.com; p136 Dudarev Mikhail; p140 Dima Sidelnikov

iStock: p28, Bischy

Endnotes

p13: Nonson, R., *Anatomy of the Soul* (p163), based on the teachings of Rebbe Nachman of Breslov (Breslov Research Institute, 1998)

p16: Epstein, G., *Healing into Immortality: A New Spiritual Medicine of Healing Stories and Imagery* (p39) (ACMI Press, 2010)

p22: Epstein, G, *Waking Dream Therapy: Unlocking the Secrets of Self Through Dreams & Imagination* (p18) (ACMI Press, 1992)

p41: From Dr Peter Reznik's article on Dream Work and personal sessions http://www.drpeterreznik.com/dreamwork

p43: From Dr Peter Reznik's article on Dream Work http://www.drpeterreznik.com/dreamwork

p106: Taylor, J, *Dream Work: Techniques for Discovering The Creative Power in Dreams* (p141) (Paulist Press, 1983)

Acknowledgments

Firstly, I'd like to thank my family. Their support was paramount to the accomplishment of this work. As always, I would like to thank all of my students and clients for their inspiration to bring forth this work. Because of them I am able to fulfill part of my potential. I am forever grateful. A very special thank you to Dr. Peter Reznik and all that came before me in this lineage, especially Colette Aboulker-Muskat. Their wisdom and inner work was instrumental for this book, not to mention the countless people I have been fortunate to share this information with on their path of healing. Thank you for all of the readers of this book who have the courage to work with dreams and deepen their connection to the imaginal realm. I want to especially thank the publishing team, most notably editors Kristine Pidkameny, Carmel Edmonds, and Clare Churly. Also thanks to illustrator Sarah Perkins and designer Sally Powell.